# HEIRS OF PAUL

# HEIRS OF PAUL
## Paul's Legacy in the New Testament and in the Church Today

J. Christiaan Beker

FORTRESS PRESS      MINNEAPOLIS

HEIRS OF PAUL

Paul's Legacy in the New Testament and in the Church Today

Scripture quotations, unless otherwise noted, are from the New Revised Standard Version of the Bible, copyright © 1989 by the Division of Christian Education of the National Council of the Churches of Christ in the United States of America.

Cover and text design: Carol Evans-Smith

**Library of Congress Cataloging-in-Publication Data**
Beker, Johan Christiaan, 1924–
    Heirs of Paul : Paul's legacy in the New Testament and in the
church today / J. Christiaan Beker.
        p.   cm.
    Includes bibliographical references and indexes.
    ISBN 0-8006-2525-0 (alk. paper)
    1. Paul, the Apostle, Saint.   2. Bible. N.T.—Criticism,
interpretation, etc.   I. Title.
BS2506.B425   1991
225.9'2—dc20                                                        91-32202
                                                                          CIP

The paper used in this publication meets the minimum requirements of American National Standard for Information Sciences—Permanence of Paper for Printed Library Materials, ANSI Z329.48-1984.

♾™

Manufactured in the U.S.A.                                AF 1-2525
95   94   93   92   91   1   2   3   4   5   6   7   8   9   10

# CONTENTS

# PREFACE

In this book I discuss an issue that concerns me deeply. After spending a considerable portion of my career on the historical-theological contours of Paul's gospel, the question suddenly arose: But what about the *reception* of Paul in the church today?

Notwithstanding our general agreement with Luther in his Preface to Romans—that Paul's letter to the Romans "is in truth the most important document in the New Testament, the gospel in its purest expression"—it is nevertheless my experience that Paul and his gospel are suffering a severe eclipse and are the least understood parts of the New Testament in the church today.

Therefore I feel it necessary to reflect on this state of affairs. And this reflection prompted me to ask the question: To what extent are Paul's *earliest interpreters* in the New Testament able to help us understand what happens to Paul's legacy in the church? Hence this book concentrates on two foci:
1. What constitutes the problem of appropriating Paul in the church today?
2. To what extent do Paul's early interpreters in the New Testament offer helpful guidelines and warning signals for contemporary appropriation of Paul? In other words, in what way do

they assist in meeting the challenge of allowing the *viva vox* of Paul's gospel to reform and re-edify the church today?

I would be remiss in not expressing my gratitude for the persons who helped me to bring this book to completion: James S. Hanson, who read the manuscript and suggested many improvements; Joseph P. Herman, who patiently and effectively retyped the manuscript several times, and finally Charles B. Puskas, for his careful editoral work.

J. C. Beker
Princeton, New Jersey

# 1

# THE PROBLEM OF PAUL'S LEGACY

## *The Focus of the Inquiry*

THE TOPIC OF "Paul and his legacy" has preoccupied scholarship for a long time. Questions about the authenticity or pseudonymity of the deutero-Pauline letters, i.e., the Pastoral Epistles (*P.E.*), Colossians, Ephesians and 2 Thessalonians continue to be debated vigorously.

Although this study assumes the pseudonymous character of these writings, the persistent debate about this matter demonstrates how clever these authors were in their imitation of Paul and to what extent they were able to appropriate Pauline tradition. Moreover, the book of Acts is as well a significant witness to the adaptation of Paul's legacy in the time after his death.[1]

Since the Reformation the primacy of Scripture over tradition has become the hallmark of Protestantism. On this issue the Reformation clashed with Roman Catholicism, which accords equal normative status to both Scripture and tradition. The primacy of Scripture in the Reformed churches was based on their conviction that the "original" apostolic witness of the New Testament was the source of all theological truth.

However, the situation changed radically with the advent of historical-critical scholarship in the nineteenth century: Scholars such as J. S. Semler and F. C. Baur argued convincingly that the traditional Protestant distinction between Scripture and tradition loses its force once it is recognized that Scripture itself is permeated by tradition. They demonstrated that in the New Testament itself the "original" witness of the apostles is supplemented by post-apostolic writers who—often under pseudonymns—transmitted and adapted the "original" apostolic testimony to the needs of their own time.

Notwithstanding the general acceptance of these fruits of historical-critical scholarship, the legacy of the Reformation, with its confessional insistence on the purity and clarity of the "original" apostolic witness, frequently compels quite a few scholars to advocate the authenticity of the deutero-Pauline letters while leading others to demote them as inferior, early Catholic misrepresentations of the historical Paul.

The quest for origins, initiated by humanism and the Reformation alike, assumed that origins signify purity and simplicity, which later literary documents perverted. For instance, early gospel-research claimed not only the priority of Mark over Matthew and Luke, but also its greater simplicity and purity in recording the words and acts of Jesus. Since a similar synoptic comparison could not be applied to Paul's letters, the search for purity often took here the form of contrasting Paul's "original" witness with its perversion and deformation by later writers—not only in the post-canonical literature (for instance, the Apostolic Fathers), but also in the post-Pauline writings of the New Testament.

However, this evaluation of Paul's legacy in the early church is heavily biased since it does not sufficiently appreciate the distinct contributions of Paul's early interpreters in the New Testament. It is therefore necessary to reconsider Paul's legacy from a new perspective. Over against those who simply contrast the "original" Paul with the so-called misrepresentations of his later interpreters, I contend that Paul's legacy can only be evaluated correctly when the claims of the original tradition (the *traditum*) are properly balanced with the claims of the adaptations that the transmission of tradition necessitates (the *traditio*).

## *Procedure*

Chapter 1 proposes that only a dual method (i.e., a comparative and a traditio-historical method) can yield a proper perspective on the adaptations of Paul by his early New Testament interpreters. It argues that only such a dual method can do justice to the claims of both the *traditum* and the *traditio*.

Chapter 2 investigates the character of the *traditum* and delineates the difficulties that Paul's gospel produces for his early interpreters in the New Testament. It suggests that the concept of adaptation is the proper mediating agent in adjudicating the claims of both the original tradition and the tradition-process. A discussion of the reception and function of Paul in the canon of the New Testament concludes this chapter.

Chapter 3 focuses on the comparative method and analyzes not only the four pseudepigraphal Pauline New Testament letters but also Luke's interpretation of Paul in the narrative of *Acts*.

Chapter 4 views the same material from another perspective. It shows the shortcomings of the comparative method and argues that the traditio-historical method gives us a more adequate insight into the adaptive strategies of Paul's early interpreters.

And finally, chapter 5 alerts the church of our time to its own urgent need of adapting Paul. It contends that an authentic proclamation of Paul's gospel today depends on the church's ability to appropriate Paul for its hearers in a new way. Moreover, it suggests that the lessons drawn from Paul's early interpreters are able to assist the church in this task.

# A Word on Method

The opinion that Paul's early New Testament interpreters represent a "fall from the true Paul" still is in vogue among many New Testament scholars. Dibelius's judgment of the "bourgeois" character of the *P.E.* has found wide acceptance[2] and is echoed by many scholars. Werner G. Kümmel, for example, speaks of "a somewhat pallid Paulinism,"[3] and Philipp Vielhauer states, "The Pastorals do not exhibit a continuation of Pauline theology, such as we find, for example, in Ephesians."[4]

## THE EXAMPLE OF THE *P.E.*

To be sure, the *P.E.* invite a comparison with Paul because they pretend to be letters of Paul, written to his two associates, Timothy and Titus. However, a comparison between Paul and the *P.E.* should not be our exclusive interest because it disregards the adaptive attempts that the author of the *P.E.* undertook to satisfy the demands of his own constituency. Indeed, scholars such as F. C. Baur, Rudolph Bultmann, and Jürgen Roloff deserve credit for recognizing this aspect of the *P.E.* Baur concludes his discussion of the *P.E.* in this way: "The glorious reputation of the apostle to the nations is not important here, but rather the fragments which the *P.E.* bring to light from the first beginnings of the Christian church, which only now begins to obtain consistent forms."[5]

And although Bultmann is quite negative about the *P.E.*, when, for example, he states in his New Testament theology that "the Christianity of the Pastorals is a somewhat faded Paulinism," he emphasizes elsewhere that the issue of authorship is "not the main issue, but rather the task is to give a positive characterization of the Pastorals."[6] Roloff supports these remarks, asserting that "the task of appreciating the Pastoral letters positively as an original literary unit within the New Testament and to understand them in terms of their theological specificity has not been achieved in any way."[7] Roloff attributes this impasse to the

ever-continuing debate about the authenticity of the letters.
While defenders of their authenticity insist on harmonizing the
letters with those of Paul, other scholars find it necessary to
radicalize the theological distance between Paul and the *P.E.* in
order to destroy the arguments of their opponents.[8]

## THE DISTINCT CHARACTER
## OF THE POST-PAULINE WRITINGS

Roloff's observation about the *P.E.* applies as well to the
other post-Pauline writings. Indeed, the issue of the theological
specificity (*Eigenart*) of these writings is much more crucial than
the problem of their authorship. The tendency of many New
Testament scholars merely to contrast Paul with the pseudepigraphal Pauline letters ignores the historical contingencies of
church life in the post-Pauline period and thus disregards the
obstacles and challenges it faced in adapting Paul's legacy. Krister
Stendahl, for instance, tends to aggravate this contrast when he
concludes his article "The Apostle Paul and the Introspective
Conscience of the West"[9] in this way: "Thus, the theologian
would note that the Pauline original should not be identified
with such interpretations . . . those catering to the problems
raised by introspection [he has especially Luther in mind]. . . .
We note how the biblical original functions as a critique of
inherited presuppositions and an incentive to new thought. Few
things are more liberating and creative in modern theology than
a clear distinction between the '*original*' and the '*translation*'
in any age, our own included."[10]

Stendahl correctly points out that, in the history of exegesis, all too frequently prior convictions and prejudices distort
the meaning of biblical texts. Nevertheless, his sharp distinction
between the original and its translation fails to recognize that
such a distinction is actually an idealistic construct. Because
Stendahl believes that the biblical scholar is able to recover the
original in its pure form, he misunderstands the necessary risks
that the interpretation of biblical texts imposes.

We must not forget that, as Søren Kierkegaard observed long ago, the recovery of "the original" can never be more than an approximation.[11] Moreover, the attempt to reconstruct the original in its pure form distances the biblical text from its present reader to such an extent that the original threatens to become an alien text. Stendahl's sharp distinction between the original and its translation is actually based on a methodological criterion that separates what it meant from what it means and thus assigns different roles to the biblical scholar ("what it meant") and to the systematic theologian ("what it means").[12]

Stendahl's proposal is defective on two counts: He fails to acknowledge (1) the biblical scholar's limited ability to recover the original ("what it meant"), and (2) the necessary changes which the transmission of tradition forces on the tradition. Indeed, since the quest for the recovery of the original cannot be separated from the demands that the necessity of adaptation imposes, all interpreters must come to terms with the problem of history—their own included. The flow of history determines not only the historical itinerary of the original but also the historicity of the interpreter.

Indeed, every translator is an interpreter unless he chooses to be simply a transliterator such as, for instance, Origen in the second volume of his Hexapla or Aquila in his Greek translation of the Old Testament. Translation is always a form of transposition. Every interpreter must face the difficulty "that sayings which originally meant one thing later on were interpreted to mean something else, something which was felt to be more relevant to human conditions of later times."[13] An interpreter, then, is involved in the business of being faithful to the old text for a new situation, which implies the implicit or the explicit transformation of the original.

The proper relation between faithfulness (cf. 1 Cor 4:2) to the old text and its transformation in a later time is difficult to measure and embraces unavoidable risks. Novelty of language cannot serve as a measure of faithfulness because it may signify either a distorted or a faithful rendering of the original tradition.

However, an interpretation becomes faithless if it simply transposes to the present a language that was meant for a bygone time and situation. In this case the original tradition becomes a frozen, dogmatic, and timeless language; it becomes traditionalist and—however sacrosanct—unintelligible. Indeed, language manifests our historicity. Unless "new" language is found, the "old" tradition cannot come to speech for new occasions. Therefore language is only faithful when the *Sachverhalt* (the material content) of the tradition can be expressed in a new *Sprachgestalt* (linguistic form). Indeed, new hermeneutical situations and fresh hearings of a text may uncover meanings that the old text did not seem to contain in its own historical context.

And yet fresh dangers arise in conjunction with these new hermeneutical situations, when, for instance, we read our own preunderstandings and ideologies into the text. The inevitable outcome of such a procedure is that the transformation of the text results in its deformation.

Thus the complex interaction between the *traditio* and the *traditum* intensifies the problems of interpretation and adaptation. As stated before, every text commences its own history of interpretation in its itinerary through time. This means that the text necessarily is transformed amid the discontinuities of history.

We can say, then, that the challenge for the adapters of the tradition consists in how to be simultaneously attentive to the claims of the original tradition and the claims of the new historical and sociocultural situations, to which the tradition intends to speak in a live manner.

Therefore we must be aware that language is an acutely historical phenomenon. Unless language adapts itself to the demands of new times and seasons, it ceases to speak and becomes unintelligible. Gerhard Ebeling makes some important remarks on this issue:

> [N]ot only does the translation [of the original text] remain imperfect with respect to the original text, always lagging behind the original, but every translation also remains a

part of the historical past, since every living language is
involved in change. The meaning of words changes, concepts [*die Begriffe*] deteriorate in the course of time, be-
coming (as we say) "worn out," having lost their earlier
capacity for expression [*Aussage-gehalt*] and the power that
was once theirs. . . . Man in this world of his, however, is
an historical man [*der geschichtliche Mensch*], caught up
with the world in constant change, a man whose present
life cannot be repeated, and who must therefore be addressed and confronted as the one he is now in his
world. . . . The only way in which we can say today, in a
strict sense, what was said in the past is to say it today in
a new and different way. . . . The sermon must be interpretation because the word of Holy Scripture is historical,
because proclamation is a historical process, and because
the man to whom proclamation is addressed is historical
along with his world. . . . Therefore theology necessarily
always finds itself involved in constant change. There can
be no *theologia perennis*, and even the historical reality of
the church is necessarily subjected to continuous change.[14]

Indeed, the historicity of language constitutes the basic
problem of the transmission of tradition. And a new appreciation
of the efforts of post-Pauline authors to shape their own distinct
theological identity in relation to the Pauline tradition cannot
succeed without some basic reflection on the nature of language
and its historicity.

## A DUAL METHOD

A dual method will be used to satisfy the claims of both
the *traditum* and the *traditio*. The comparative component of
the method must determine the extent to which Paul's early
interpreters were able to do justice to the claims of Paul's original
gospel. The traditio-historical component of the method must
determine how these interpreters adapted Paul's gospel as a living
and relevant voice to the new historical circumstances of their
time.

The dual method, then, seeks to avoid the excesses either of absolutizing the comparative method to the neglect of the traditio-historical method or of absolutizing the traditio-historical method at the cost of the other. Indeed, an exclusive focus on the traditio-historical method embraces the proposition that Christianity *is* whatever it *becomes* in the tradition.[15] According to this view, the process of tradition necessarily authorizes the loss of an authentic Christian identity with the result that Christianity has no distinctive character of its own.

Again, notwithstanding the necessary critical task of the comparative method to safeguard the adequacy of the adaptive process, an exclusive focus on the comparative method would involve readers in an ahistorical and docetic conception of the church in its complex itinerary through history. For in this case we would disregard the church's necessity to adapt the tradition in accordance with the demands and needs of its particular location in history.

# 2

# BASIC ISSUES IN THE TRANSMISSION OF TRADITION

## *The Traditum: The Problem Inherent in Paul's Gospel*

The problems posed by the gospel of Paul underscore the difficulties that his early interpreters in the New Testament had to face in their attempts to adapt his legacy.

Therefore an inquiry into the character of Paul's *traditum* (the original tradition) must precede the investigation of the *traditio* (the tradition-process; see p. 27ff., below).

### PAUL'S METHOD AND MESSAGE

There is general consensus in recent New Testament scholarship as to the central problem of interpreting Paul's letters. Hendrikus Boers, for instance, argues that the identification of a center that integrates the diversity of the apostle's thinking into a coherent whole is the most fundamental problem in Pauline interpretation.[1] And others agree with this assessment; Hans Hübner, for example, states that "the theme of contradictions in Paul requires an urgent solution."[2] There are at least five factors that impede the recovery of the center of Paul's thought: (1) Paul did not write a "dogmatics in outline" as, for example, Melanchthon thought when he called Romans a "*compendium doctrinae Christianae.*" Moreover, Paul did not compose philosophical letter-essays (as, e.g., Seneca) or leave us with an essay entitled "How I Changed My Mind," nor did he even delineate his thought patterns in a logical, sequential manner. Far from being a systematic theologian, Paul was an interpreter of the gospel that he had inherited from the church at Antioch after his conversion and call to the apostolate.

(2) Furthermore, Paul was not a thinker whose originality and creativity manifested itself in the doctrinal architecture of his writings or in the form of soliloquies and meditations in the manner of Marcus Aurelius's private diary (*to eis heauton*). All we possess from him are seven occasional letters, written at different times for widely different occasions and exhibiting a great variety of thought.

A series of such occasional letters makes it difficult to inquire into the center of Paul's thought. Moreover, we cannot ascertain with any precision the thoughts and rejoinders of his addressees since the efforts of "mirror reading" produce uncertain results.[3]

(3) These negative observations lead us to the crux of the matter: Paul's method of interpreting the gospel resists our attempts to establish the "fixed core" of his thought. Since there is no *theologia perennis* in Paul, the transmission of a dogmatic Paul to later historical periods amounts to a misrepresentation of his thought. This is true because Paul's hermeneutic of the gospel is so determined by the contingent situations he addresses that the coherent and abiding elements of his gospel cannot be abstracted from their interplay with these various contingencies. The intensely personal and dialogical character of Paul's gospel demonstrates that the written form of his letters is actually a substitute for the viva vox of his personal presence. Paul, then, continuously attempts to make the abiding word of the gospel a "word on target" for his audience so that the gospel comes to

people "not in word only, but also in power and in the Holy Spirit and with full conviction" (1 Thess 1:5).

(4) Moreover, the rhetorical situations that Paul creates in his letters constitute a further obstacle in establishing a fixed core of his thought since the implied situations may occasionally be at variance with the actual situation to which he responds. In other words, we must pay attention to the close interrelationships between Paul's thought, his argumentative strategies, and his attempts to persuade his audiences so that they will choose his side.

(5) Our recovery and appropriation of the "original Paul" is made all the more difficult because of a feature of his thought that has thus far received little attention. It concerns the passionate nature of the apostle's personality, which affects not only his life-style but also the texture of his thought.

Jonathan Edwards, in his *Religious Affections*, puts forward the thesis that "true religion, in great part, consists of holy affections." D. M. Yeager comments: "This is to say that it belongs to the domain of will, where will-as-desire is experienced with uncommon intensity. Edwards holds that 'God has imbued the soul with two faculties,' the speculative understanding that perceives and considers things and the faculty of inclination that approves/accepts or opposes/rejects that which the soul in its other faculty merely views and considers. Inclination governs the direction of understanding, and it necessarily governs all action."[4]

Yeager detects a similar emphasis in William James's *The Will to Believe*: "The will to believe is not a resolute voluntary act; the will to believe is a revolutionary passion."[5] According to James, "we not only *may* consult our passional longings, but we *must* consult our passional longings."[6] And Yeager comments: "James has advanced to a peculiar stage of self-consciousness in which it is not enough to have 'simple faith' . . . because the question is not whether one might have that but whether, having it, one dares to trust it, to give oneself up to it, to embrace it in the confidence that it at least might be 'prophetic and right' rather than delusive and self-betraying."[7]

Edwards's "holy affections" and James's notion of the "passional nature," i.e., the positive role that passions perform in all our activities, helps us to understand not only the affective nature of Paul's thinking, but also our difficulty in recovering and transmitting his thought. Jerome, at least, had a sense for Paul's passionate thinking when he commented on Paul's letters: "*non verba sed tonitrua*," (i.e., he hears "the thunder" when he reads "the words").[8] It is not intended here to explore the psychoanalytic dimensions of Paul's soul or the psychological components of Paul's passionate zeal as reported, for instance, in Acts and in Galatians. According to Acts, Paul is engaged in "breathing threats and murder against the disciples of the Lord" (Acts 9:1), and Paul himself reports in Galatians: "You have heard, no doubt, of my earlier life in Judaism. I was violently persecuting the church of God and was trying to destroy it. I advanced in Judaism beyond many among my people of the same age, for I was far more zealous for the traditions of my ancestors" (Gal 1:13-14).

The interest in this study lies in the intricate interaction between Paul's cognitive and affective thought patterns. In this context we must remember that the Paul transmitted to us by the canon and the history of doctrine is essentially a doctrinal Paul, which means that attention has almost exclusively focused on his cognitive endowment and logical argument. And this legacy of a cognitive-doctrinal Paul still monopolizes New Testament scholarship whenever it interprets Paul in terms of dogmatic topics or in terms of a fixed doctrinal core.

However, we fail to understand Paul unless we attend to the delicate balance in his thought between "speculative understanding" and "the faculty of inclination" (see Edwards). If it is true that "inclination" and "holy affections" govern the orientation of our understanding and necessarily direct all our action, a new way of understanding Paul has become possible.

Indeed, Paul's passionate thinking originates in his apostolic call (1 Cor 9:1; Gal 1:12), which he believes to have granted him direct access to God's revelation. His call has a visionary and auditory character. Henceforth Paul's life is marked by the power of the Spirit, which manifests itself in his pneumatic ecstasy and guides his spiritual understanding (1 Cor 2:7-16). And yet Paul's passion is not simply an outburst of self-serving pneumatic exuberance. Rather his passion is the passion of compassion. Paul demonstrates at several occasions that the passion of pneumatic immediacy has no value unless it serves the compassion of sober intelligibility. This is nowhere more clearly expressed than in 2 Cor 5:13: "For if we are beside ourselves, it is for God; if we are in our right mind [*Le Bible de Jerusalem*: '*raisonnables*'], it is for you." And this sober "reasonableness" is motivated by Paul's concern for the "upbuilding" (*oikodomē*) of the church (confer esp. 1 Corinthians 14).

It seems, then, that in the face of these difficulties a dead end has been reached in our effort to understand more clearly the method and message of Paul's gospel. How can we hope to understand the intricate interplay between coherence and contingency and between thought and passion in his gospel when Paul does not impose a fixed doctrinal system on his audience, refuses to yield to opportunistic devices in order to please his hearers and, moreover, frequently allows intuitive passion to short-circuit the logic of his argument?

The problem becomes more acute when we realize that it is impossible to divorce or abstract the coherence of Paul's gospel from its interface with contingent circumstances or to construe the relation between coherence and contingency in a casuistic manner. Indeed, casuistic procedures apply fixed and normative bodies of teaching to a host of contingent situations as, for instance, in the interpretive methods of Judaism and Christian orthodoxy. Judaism views the Law of Moses as an eternally given and fixed literary document that Mishna, Midrash, and Talmud must try to apply to new historical circumstances. Similarly, Christian orthodoxy regards its fixed creedal and dogmatic confessions as sacred texts, which become normative for every new contingent situation.

Since passionate thinking is part and parcel of Paul's theologizing, it plays an important role in solving the problem of Paul's method and message. Paul's method of interweaving coherence and contingency is to a large extent determined by his affective-cognitive dialectic, which we can frequently discern in his letters. Sometimes profound empathy and coherent logic prevail (confer Rom 5:12-21; 8:18-30; 1 Thess 2:1-8; Phil 1:1-26); other times passionate impatience, irrational outbursts, nonsequiturs and breakdowns of the original sentence construction (*anakoloutha*) interrupt his argument. Thus it is not surprising that Paul's passionate thinking evokes in us mixed reactions: He is apt both to irritate us in his overbearing and dogmatic manner, and at the same time appeal to us as a committed, caring, and sensitive pastor.

If there is any truth to the truisms that genius does not tolerate mediocrity and that there is no power without passion, then Paul seems to confirm both. On the one hand his passion is transparent, when, for example, he defines the gospel as a "power for salvation" (Rom 1:16), and when he uses violent military imagery in declaring that "the weapons of our warfare are not merely human, but they have divine power to destroy strongholds" (2 Cor 10:4)[9] or when he speaks "like a madman" (2 Cor 11:23). On the other hand, this passionate commitment shifts into profundity of thought when, for instance, he disarms with a stroke of genius the petty complaints of the Corinthians about his vacillation in making travel plans, i.e., his supposed yes and no, by referring to the fundamental yes of the gospel (2 Cor 1:15-20).

## THE CENTER OF PAUL'S THOUGHT

The difficulties of delineating with any precision the center of Paul's thought cannot be resolved easily. Indeed, the problem between coherence and contingency in his thought cannot be construed as the relation between abstract principle and its concrete applicability. The flexibility of the relation between coherence and contingency is such that the coherent center of Paul's gospel can only be grasped in its particularity. Therefore the adaptation of Paul's gospel to different times, altered world-views and new sociocultural conditions remains a hazardous and risky undertaking.

Nevertheless, two observations are in order here:

1. The difficulty of defining the center of Paul's thought with any precision does not prevent us from sketching the basic contours of his thought as long as we are aware that this can only be done in an abstract way, i.e., on the level of a second order of thought.

2. It is necessary to distinguish the ability of the historian to achieve a proximate delineation of the basic contours of Paul's thought from the hermeneutical problem of the adaptation of his thought to new times and circumstances.

The following attempt to sketch the basic contours of Paul's thought is undertaken with these observations in mind.

It is clear that the fabric of Paul's theology is permeated by an apocalyptic substrate. His thinking strains forward to the coming apocalyptic triumph of God, when everything in creation that resists his majesty will be overcome and the whole creation will be at peace in being embraced by the everlasting arms of God.

The theocentric cast of Paul's thought is an inherent part of his apocalyptic hope. In other words, Paul's Christology is subordinated to the coming triumph of God. Indeed, he reiterates throughout his letters the refrain of the triumph of God, for instance, in Rom 11:36: "For from him and through him and to him are all things. To him be glory forever. Amen."[10]

The specific Christian character of the apocalyptic substructure of Paul's thought is evident when he proclaims the death and resurrection of Christ as God's apocalyptic intervention. This act of God creates a radical dualism between the old word and God's new world in Christ, which permeates Paul's anthropology, soteriology, and ethic. The apocalyptic power structures of his thought, embodied in the antithetical powers of death and life, give rise to a *"Kontrast-denken"* (Jost Eckert) or, as E. P. Sanders formulates it, "a thinking in black and white," which rarely allows mediating positions. Indeed, the powers of death, sin, the law, and the flesh, which oppose the reign of God in Christ, generate Paul's radical anthropological, soteriological, and ethical convictions. No mediation is possible between the law and Christ, between the works of the law and faith, or between the flesh and the Spirit. Moreover, since sin is an enslaving power and not an occasional transgression, the meaning of redemption is not exhausted by the notion of the forgiveness of sins and the atonement of past transgressions but rather is defined in terms of "a new creation."[11]

Paul's christological apocalyptic also pervades his ethic. Since Christians live in the interim between God's act in Christ and his theophany in final judgment, they are required to give an account of their moral life at the hour of the final judgment, "so that each may receive recompense for what has been done in the body, whether good or evil" (2 Cor 5:10).

Finally, Paul's gospel is shaped by its encounter with Judaism. His struggle with his Jewish heritage penetrates all the aspects of his thought. Its affective-cognitive dimensions are nowhere more evident than in his reflections on Israel's role in God's plan of salvation, especially in his "great sorrow and unceasing anguish" (Rom 9:2) and in his "heart's desire and prayer to God for them . . . that they may be saved" (Rom 10:1). His perplexity about Israel's rejection of Christ, about its "being ignorant of the righteousness that comes from God" (Rom 10:3) and about its present hardening (Rom 11:7-10, 25; 9:18) is only relieved for him when he recalls God's abiding election of Israel (Rom 11:29) and knows that Israel will be saved at the eschatological hour (Rom 11:26).

## THE INTERPRETIVE DIFFICULTIES

When we remember the difficulties brought about by the contingent location of Paul's method and message—the occasional and personal character of Paul's letters, with their passionate intensity, their dialogical style, their rhetorical argument, and contingent-specific features—it comes as no surprise that his early New Testament interpreters frequently stumbled in their adaptations of Paul's gospel. These obstacles become all the more pronounced when compared with the seemingly limitless adaptive possibilities afforded by narrative literature such as the gospels. In contrast to occasional letters, narratives have a much more intelligible and coherent structure. Readers of a story can interpret it in a deliberative and reflective manner. The sequential flow of the narrative, its character development, its plot and reversal allow readers to read the whole in terms of the parts and the parts in terms of the whole. Moreover, a storyteller is able to create metaphors that evoke multiple layers of the story and allow the reader to participate directly in the story at various levels.

Paul, however, is not a storyteller, but the man of apodictic-performative speech, the man of the argument and the concept. While a story unfolds, a concept defines; a story is multidimensional, the concept singular; the story opens up horizons for imaginative participation, whereas the concept delimits a specific boundary for thought. Furthermore, in contrast to the language of narrative, Paul's conceptual langage is an obstacle to direct religious appropriation, since concepts and arguments must be understood before they can be appropriated. The reader of a letter of Paul must often guess what a specific argument is all about and to whom it is directed.

Finally, the contingent aspects of the letters of Paul are much more pronounced in their situational particularity than the gospels because the gospels—notwithstanding their address to particular Christian regions—possess a much more catholic character.

# The Traditio: *The Problem Inherent in the Transmission of Paul's Gospel*

It has become clear that the transmission of Paul's gospel to subsequent historical periods is fraught with difficulties. Both his contingent method of interweaving coherence and contingency and the passionate character of his thought have always caused severe problems for the adaptation of his gospel. For instance, the church fathers of the patristic period could only transmit Paul's gospel by severing and isolating its coherence from its situation-specific contingency. Thus faithfulness to Paul consisted chiefly in borrowing either some of his moral injunctions or some of his theological vocabulary, as if they possessed universal applicability and could be transmitted without regard for their contingent contextuality. This procedure could only pervert Paul's method and message. It led to a domestication of Paul, which was bolstered by the need of the patristic church to harmonize Paul's message with that of the other apostles of the New Testament canon (see below, pp. 31–34). Moreover, the popularity of Paul's letters among gnostic groups in the second century A.D. compelled the church to claim Paul for its own orthodoxy by means of several normative apostolic criteria, i.e., by an apostolic canon, an apostolic rule of faith (*regula fidei/regula veritatis*) and an apostolic interpretation (the episcopate).

Notwithstanding these attempts to save Paul for the church, he was largely silenced by the apologists,[11] and this neglect lasted practically until the time of Augustine.

However, it would be wrong to think that the problem of the transmission of Paul's gospel first arose in and was limited to the patristic period. As we shall see, it is an acute problem not only for Paul's early interpreters in New Testament times, but also for every subsequent period in church history. In fact, it is still with us today because we continue to treat Paul as an abstract-propositional, dogmatic thinker. Indeed, the lasting legacy of Paul's adaptation in the long history of the church consists in the transformation of Paul, the passionate thinker into Paul, the dogmatician. Most of us perpetuate the custom of reading Paul in an ahistorical manner by universalizing some of his theological idiom while ignoring its sociohistorical setting.

Therefore the issue of the transmission of Paul's gospel requires an urgent solution. How shall we transmit the historical specificity of his gospel to different worldviews and later times? For instance, is it possible to translate for our time Paul's doctrine of justification or the time-bound apocalyptic elements of his gospel with their imminent expectation of the parousia? Or how do we adapt the intricacies of his culturally determined arguments about the Torah and Israel? Is it not true that many so-called central Pauline doctrines and arguments have become largely irrelevant and unintelligible to us since they fail to connect with the needs and problems of contemporary life? (see below, pp. 99–104)

Indeed, the central issue here is the historical particularity of Paul's gospel because it involves all the other issues that his gospel raises for us. We are genuinely perplexed today why Paul's gospel—once the glorious centerpiece of the Reformation with its revolutionary and liberating message—has become so alien to us and evokes so much hostility, especially because of its many culturally determined pronouncements concerning, for example, the status of women, slavery, marriage, sex, or homosexuality.

The problem of adapting Paul's gospel for our time can be solved only when we face squarely the issue of the inevitable historicity of human life and language. As Ebeling has so clearly seen (see p. 15–16, above), history brings about basic changes in language and transforms profoundly the meanings of concepts and syntax. Indeed, the historicity of language constitutes the basic problem for the transmission of tradition. Therefore, we will be unable to appreciate the efforts of post-Pauline authors in the New Testament to shape their own distinct theological identity in relation to the Pauline tradition unless we seriously reflect on the nature of language and its historicity. Thus, the investigation of the transmission of tradition must be sensitive to the findings of social history and comparative linguistics in its effort to ascertain whether and how the "old" tradition can function in a relevant way for new historical and sociocultural contexts.

## THE CONCEPT OF ADAPTATION

The concept of adaptation is a helpful tool in exploring the dynamics of the transmission of tradition. We may define

its role as that of a mediating agent between the necessary claims
of the original tradition and the claims of the new sociohistorical
location to which the original tradition must speak. In other
words, it mediates between the double meaning that inheres in
the concept "tradition," i.e., the *traditum* (the deposit of the
tradition) and the *traditio* (the transmission of tradition).

In its role as mediator, adaptation rejects not only an
artificial and outmoded repristination of the *traditum*, i.e., the
"old" tradition, but also the willful distortion of the "old" tradition for the sake of so-called modern, up-to-date neologisms
and ideological interests.

Thus such mediation is unavoidable when the original
tradition is not considered to be an archaeological deposit of
the past but rather a normative word for the present. In this
context we must be aware that the concept of adaptation functions on two distinct levels: temporal and spatial.

On the *temporal* level adaptation seeks to bridge the time
gap between the original tradition and its new location in history,
while on the *spatial* level it endeavors to adapt the tradition to
new sociocultural situations.

Since it is the task of adaptation to transmit the tradition
(the *traditio* of the *traditum*) on both a temporal-diachronic and
a sociocultural-synchronic level, resistance to adaptation necessarily produces ahistorical and docetic forms of the transmission of the tradition. Indeed, it is the mark of docetism to simply
disregard the historicity of all tradition. For instance, when fundamentalism insists on the binding and normative authority of
the written word of Scripture for our time, or when theologians
attribute timeless normative truth to a canon within the canon
in the New Testament, they are both guilty of a docetic interpretation of the tradition.

## THE LIMITS OF ADAPTATION

To be sure, we must be attentive to the dangers to which
the method of adaptation is liable. Adaptation can easily trans-
gress its proper boundaries and lapse into forms of anachronism

and/or acculturation. Such transgressions occur, for example, when adaptation disregards the claim of the original tradition and either deforms it for the sake of its own timely interpretation (anachronism) or coalesces it with the taste of the culture, which it seeks to serve (acculturation). However, even more severe forms of anachronism and acculturation result from a refusal to engage in adaptation. In such cases the original tradition is simply imposed on later times as if there were no intervening history and development.

Thus, a proper adaptation will always seek to safeguard the claims of the original tradition, but in such a way as to transpose the original tradition (its *Sachverhalt*) into a fresh symbolic language, which is appropriate to its new historical location (its *Sprachgestalt*).

Adaptation, then, is risky business and requires from its performers sensitivity and imagination as to how authenticity and relevance are to be adjudicated.

The extent to which the early interpreters of Paul in the New Testament were able to do justice to the claims of Paul's gospel will be the focus of the discussion in chapter 3. Subsequently in chapter 4 these writings will be viewed from a different perspective and the adaptive skills of these interpreters will be appraised in terms of the claims that their historical situations demanded from them.

# The Historical Paul and the Canonical Paul

The method by which the framers of the New Testament canon adapted Paul illustrates how the historical Paul could become the canonical Paul.

## THE ADAPTIVE METHOD OF THE FRAMERS OF THE CANON

Since Paul's letters created a difficult problem for the framers of the canon, it is important to understand the factors that determined their method. Nils Dahl states the problem succinctly: "The theological problem raised by the Pauline epistles was not their plurality, but their particularity."[13]

The particularity of Paul's gospel was felt to be a problem at the time of the canonization of the Pauline letters toward the end of the second century A.D. Because the "apostolic" witness of the canon claimed a universal address, the framers of the canon decreed that the letters of Paul, just like the Catholic Epistles, had been addressed to all Christian churches. After all, canonicity meant catholicity. For how could the "apostolic" witness be applicable to the catholic church if Paul had only written to some specific churches about specific problems?

Although Oscar Cullmann argues that the particularity of the "apostolic" letters in the canon did not create as severe a problem as the plurality of the four Gospels, we must remember that plurality and particularity produce similar problems. How can the unity and universality of the one apostolic gospel be maintained when the plurality of the Gospels belies their unity, and when the particularity of Paul's letters militates against the universality of his gospel? To be sure, the early church was especially preoccupied with the plurality of the Gospels. For instance, Tatian's harmony of the four Gospels into one (the *Diatessaron*) enjoyed wide popularity in the church, especially in Syria, until it was rejected by Irenaus (born about 180 A.D.) Irenaus, in turn, attempted to solve the problem of both the plurality of the Gospels and the particularity of Paul's letters by arguing that, just as the unity of the Gospels was based on the universal number four, the universality of Paul's letters rested as well on the universal number seven because Paul had written to seven churches. At the same time the Muratorian Canon stipulated that "the Pauline letters are accepted by the church catholic" (*in catholica habentur* 1.69).

In other words, the framers of the canon attempted to solve the issue of the particularity of Paul's letters by positing their universal, "catholic" relevance, and so defused their occasional character. We must be aware that this solution had far-reaching consequences. It disregarded not only the contingent character of Paul's interpretation of the gospel within the multiple contexts of his various letters, but also the particularity of Paul's interpretation of the gospel compared with the other "apostolic" witnesses of the canon. Thus the trajectory of Paul's letters from their early collection to their canonical shape was marked by an increasing harmonization of them with the rest of the canon. The result of this harmonization was the obfuscation of what was most characteristic about Paul's gospel, i.e., its contingent character.

Dahl correctly blames the Muratorian Canon for its false assumption "that the canonicity and catholicity of the epistles can be stressed only at the expense of their particularity." And he continues: "To the apostle himself, letters to particular churches written for special occasions were the proper literary form for making theological statements. Of this fact both exegesis and theology, not to mention preaching, have to take account. The particularity of the Pauline epistles points to the historicalness of all theology, even that of an apostle."[14]

Thus, the docetic and generalizing propensities of the framers of the canon actually produced a "catholic" Paul who not only was in harmony with the other "apostolic" witnesses in the canon, but also had taught a uniform doctrine to all his churches.

## THE INFLUENCE OF THE "CATHOLIC" PAUL

We must be aware how profoundly the portrait of this "catholic" Paul has influenced the interpretation of the apostle throughout the course of church history. Indeed, the creation of this "catholic" Paul became a great stumbling block in the recovery of the historical Paul. For the Paul who was accepted in the canon was actually a synthetic Paul, a mixture composed from his letters, from the post-Pauline writings, and from legendary stories based on oral tradition. And even after the Reformation rediscovered the "original" Paul for the church and its theology, it never questioned the harmonious witness that

Paul and (most of) the other New Testament witnesses supposedly shared.[15]

Moreover, the insistence of the Reformation on the doctrinal unity and all-sufficiency of Scripture in its struggle against
the Roman Catholic doctrine of the coequality of Scripture and
tradition finally obscured the particularity of Paul's gospel and
his hermeneutic: Protestant orthodoxy simply transmitted the
catholic Paul of the New Testament canon as doctrinal authority
for the church.

Henceforth the search for the substance and center of
Paul's thought became a search for its timeless dogmatic truth.
This process continued basically until the rise of historical-critical scholarship in the eighteenth and nineteenth centuries (see
J. S. Semler; F. C. Baur). In other words, the portrait of Paul as
a dogmatic theologian won the day, while his letters became
proof texts to undergird Protestant doctrine. Thus, whatever
empathy the framers of the canon deserve for their attempt to
solve the "Pauline problem," their adaptation of Paul was fatally
flawed.

At this point in the discussion it becomes necessary to
inquire whether the precanonical period, i.e., the period of Paul's
early interpreters in the New Testament, already foreshadows
the destiny of Paul's gospel in the postcanonical period. In what
measure were these interpreters able to maintain the contingent
particularity of Paul's gospel, and to what extent did they simply
succumb to the historical and theological constraints that im-
pinged on the framers of the canon?

# 3

## THE HISTORICAL PAUL AND HIS NEW TESTAMENT INTERPRETERS: A COMPARATIVE APPROACH

THIS ANALYSIS OF Paul's New Testament interpreter (i.e., the *P. E.*,[1] Acts, Colossians, Ephesians and 2 Thessalonians) discusses the *P.E.* in conjunction with *Acts* because these two writings share common features, notwithstanding their different perspectives on Paul. Again, Colossians and Ephesians are coordinated because of Ephesians's proximity to and dependence on Colossians. The analytical part of this investigation is concluded with a discussion of 2 Thessalonians, which in style and content occupies a unique place among the Pauline pseudepigrapha.

This chapter concentrates on a comparison of Paul with his later New Testament interpreters to determine their ability to do justice to the claims of his gospel, i.e., to appropriate Paul correctly.

Subsequently, the same material will be approached from a different perspective in chapter 4. There, in accordance with the dual method (see p. 16, above), the comparative component will be complemented with a traditio-historical component to achieve proper balance between the two approaches. The traditio-historical method must explore the problems and challenges that the early New Testament interpreters of Paul faced in their endeavor to adapt Paul for the needs of their own time. This dual perspective on the adaptation of Paul's gospel is adopted not only to rebut the theory of "the fall from the true Paul"— which scholars so frequently apply to Paul's early New Testament interpreters—but also to bring about an appreciation for the difficult task these early interpreters faced. Moreover, it will be shown that such a dual perspective is not simply an academic-historical enterprise; we must recognize that their successes and failures in this endeavor constitute important precedents for the church today because they alert the church to the dangers and opportunities that accompany its own task of adapting Paul to our time.

## *Paul's Legacy in the Pastoral Epistles*

K. M. Fischer characterizes the second half of the first century A.D. as "the era of the New Testament Pseudepigraphy."[2] He bases this judgment on the fact that between the time of the Pauline letters and the end of the first century A.D. no early-Christian writing carries the name of its true author, but that instead apostolic names are used as pseudonyms.

### PAUL'S PORTRAIT IN THE PASTORAL EPISTLES

Fischer's characterization applies certainly to the *P.E.*: they are a collection of three letters that were written around the same time (the end of the first century A.D.), never circulated separately, and were ostensibly addressed to churches in Ephesus and Crete to assist church leaders in their task of preaching, guidance, and organizational planning. The letters' pseudonymity is twofold, involving both the author and addressees: They are supposedly written by Paul to two of his most intimate co-workers, Timothy and Titus, who are located respectively in Ephesus and on Crete.

The letters' claim to authority is based on the apostle Paul and his teaching and—what is more—it is based exclusively on Paul's authority. In other words, legitimate Christianity and the authoritative gospel are identified solely with the gospel of Paul. In contrast to Luke-Acts, there is no appeal to other apostolic leaders or to the Jerusalem authorities. Indeed *Acts* grounds the validity of the gospel for the Gentiles on the decision of the apostolic college in Jerusalem (15:1-29) and emphasizes the harmonious unity of the church and its common devotion "to the apostles' teaching and fellowship" (2:42).

In other words, the Pastor conveys to his churches the unique authority of Paul and wants to maintain the continuity of Paul's gospel amid the discontinuities of a different era. He writes after Paul's death when Paul could no longer be present nor his viva vox be heard.

The twofold pseudonymity of his letters, then, serves an important purpose: Attribution to Paul guarantees the continuity of the apostolic tradition in the time after the apostle's death. In this context the fictive name of Paul is crucial because "Paul" gives these letters their authoritative stature. Indeed, just as in the authentic letters of Paul the name of the sender in the pre-script undergirds Paul's personal authority and establishes the authoritative claim of his letters, so the name of Paul functions likewise for the Pastor, a feature that the close similarity of the *P.E.* to the form of Paul's letters confirms.

Moreover, whenever the historical Paul was forced to be absent from his churches, he used to maintain contact with them by means of letters and/or coworkers. Thus it was natural for his later interpreters to continue this practice after Paul's death, i.e., after his permanent absence. In this way pupils of Paul were able to transmit the authority of the apostle by means of letters written in the name of Paul.

The figure of Paul is inextricably bound up with the reputation of the apostle in the area of Asia Minor where the *P.E.* were written. Since they are addressed to churches that were directly or indirectly the fruit of Paul's missionary labor, their portrait of Paul is heavily influenced by the historical impact of the apostle. Indeed, the impact both of Paul's letters and of his missionary work did contribute to his exclusive authority. In other words, while the author seems to have known those letters of Paul, which circulated in the regions of Asia Minor (especially Romans, 1 Corinthians, and Philippians),[3] Paul's portrait in the *P.E.* is actually a composite of literary references, legends, stories, and anecdotes.

Indeed, we must remember that various traditions combined to create Paul's portrait in the post-apostolic period: "Paul's portrait is here the reflection of the way in which the tradition has formed it. The readers saw before them 'the whole Paul, as they imagined him' (Adolf Jülicher, *Einleitung*, 172) and that was not simply the historical Paul, but the Paul who spoke to a post-Pauline era. Although the Pastoral Epistles were not directly written by Paul, they indicate the way in which a later generation saw and revered Paul."[4]

Thus the *P.E.* demonstrate the considerable distance between the historical Paul and the Paul of the *P.E.* This is confirmed by other features of Paul's portrait. For instance, the Paul of the *P.E.* has become such an established authority that a simple appeal to his words and admonitions suffices to silence all questions and arguments. We detect here the impact of the transmission of tradition in the post-Pauline period: Paul has now become "the great Paul" whose reputation and missionary success everyone in the church must acknowledge. In fact, Paul has achieved such an exclusive status that he simply argues *from* his unquestionable authority to a submissive church rather than being forced to argue *for* it against his detractors in his churches as the historical Paul was forced to do.

The historical distance between Paul and the Paul of the *P.E.* manifests itself in another significant feature of these letters. Paul's polemic with the Torah and Judaism is no longer a live issue in the *P.E.* The confrontation with Judaism—so prominent in Paul, Luke-Acts, Mark, Matthew, and John—is a thing of the past and has ceased to be a concern for the Paul of the *P.E.*

Indeed, the churches of the *P.E.* are largely made up of Gentiles and are seemingly alienated from the Jewish roots of Christianity. In fact, the conflict of the historical Paul with his Jewish and Judaizing opponents is here replaced by a Paul who must combat Jewish-gnostic heretics within the church.

The characteristic features of Paul's portrait in the *P.E.* become even clearer when we compare them with the portrait of Paul in Acts. Although the *P.E.* and Acts both draw their picture of Paul from various legends and narratives that circulated in Paul's missionary territories in Asia Minor and Greece, their use of Paul's letters differs radically. Whereas the *P.E.* cite and allude to them extensively, Acts ignores them completely. Thus, although the *P.E.* are, like Acts, dependent on traditions about Paul, the *P.E.*, unlike Acts, are also indebted to the thought of Paul. Accordingly, the exclusivity of Paul's authority in the *P.E.* sharply contrasts with its portrayal in Acts where Paul is denied apostolic status and where his message is smoothly harmonized with that of the Jerusalem apostles.

## THE RELATION OF "PAUL'S" METHOD TO HIS MESSAGE

Important differences between the Paul of the authentic letters and the Paul of the *P.E.* surface when we compare Paul's structure of argumentation (his method) and the material content of his thought (his message) with their representation in the *P.E.*

*The Method.* The intricate and flexible manner in which the historical Paul integrates the coherence of his gospel with the various contingent situations of his missionary churches (see pp. 20, 23, above) undergoes a profound change. Since Paul does not sever the coherence of the gospel from its contingent applicability, their relationship never becomes a matter of imposing casuistically a fixed body of authoritative teaching on the situation at hand.

Indeed, Paul's ability to interweave coherence and contingency in a flexible manner conforms to the dialogical character of his hermeneutic. Paul's rhetoric, with its polemical and per-suasive strategies, shows the lively presence of his partners in the dialogue both when they demand clarifications and when they radically oppose Paul. For instance, Paul is regularly engaged in defending his apostolic status against those who either dispute his apostolic status altogether (2 Corinthians) or indict him for falsely claiming an independent apostolic status (Galatians).

In the *P.E.*, however, the lively dialogical structure of Paul's argumentation has collapsed. Paul's exclusive authority and the undisputed validity of his teaching demonstrate how the tradition brings about an increasing "depersonalization" and "dehistoricization" of the apostle. Roloff characterizes the post-canonical era in these terms: "While in the biblical writings of the second generation the apostles are still portrayed as concrete historical figures in the context of a historical tradition, now the apostles become objects of mythization (*Mythisierung*), collec-tivization (*Kollectivierung*) and legendary imagination (*Legen-dalisierung*)."[5]

In this manner Ignatius portrays the apostles as a heavenly council that symbolically represents the order of the church: "likewise let all respect the deacons as Jesus Christ, even as the bishop is also a type of the Father, and the presbyters as the council of God and the college of apostles" (Trall. 3:1, see also Magn 6:1); likewise 1 Clement and Polycarp present the apostles as one undifferentiated unity (1 Clem 42:1; 44:1; Polycarp, Phil 9:1), whereas the apocryphal *Acts of the Apostles* describes them as fantastic miracle workers and global missionaries.

Although the *P.E.* do not exhibit a heavy *Legendalisierung* of this sort, the movement toward such a legendary portrait of Paul is under way. Dehistoricization takes here the form of pre-senting Paul basically as a static and dogmatic person, notwith-standing the personal features of Paul's portrait in 2 Timothy. Throughout the *P.E.* Paul is portrayed as a figure who imposes doctrine and engages in monologue. The Pauline gospel has now become a "deposit of truth" (*parathēkē*; 1 Tim 6:20; 2 Tim 1:14) and "sound doctrine" (*hygiainousa didaskalia*; 1 Tim 1:10; 2 Tim 4:3). Indeed, the Paul of the *P.E.* does not take the theological claims of his opponents seriously, but rather vilifies and stereotypes them as empty hotheads and moral perverts (for instance, "men, depraved in mind and bereft of the truth" [1 Tim 6:5]; "evil men and impostors" [2 Tim 3:13]; "idle talkers and deceivers" [Titus 1:10]). Thus, Paul's dialogical method of interweaving coherence and contingency is displaced in the *P.E.* by a bifurcation of coherence and contingency because the timeless, rigid, and abstract character of the coherence of the gospel is unable to relate itself properly to the challenges of the contingent situation. Moreover, the contingency of the situation is here frivolously misrepresented, caricatured, and not deemed worthy of serious rebuttal.

*The Message*

The bifurcation of coherence and contingency affects not only the author's method of argumentation, but also his presentation of Paul's message. Because the author intends to be faithful to Paul and to Paul alone as the paradigm and prototype of Christian truth (see Paul as *prōtos* and *hypotypōsis,* 1 Tim 1:16; see 2:7; 2 Tim 1:11-12), references to Paul's terminology and conceptuality abound, along with frequent allusions to his letters.[6]

However, the author's abundant use of Paul's terminology must not deceive us. The bifurcation of coherence and contingency produces a linguistic structure that petrifies Paul's dynamic coherent language and thus relates itself only artificially to its contingent situation. In fact Paul's concepts have now become sacrosanct and "holy" words to which the tradition has given a fixed and frozen meaning. And so they have lost their dynamic interrelation with the particular contingent situation in and for which they originally functioned.

Once again, the influence of the transmission of tradition makes itself felt here (see pp. 29–30, above). The inevitable historicity of language and of language patterns gives rise to considerable changes in the meaning of traditional words and concepts, which must now function within a very different theological and sociohistorical context.

Indeed, the author's appeal to the specificity of Paul's gospel is deflected by a worldview that differs sharply from that of Paul's time. The author is much more at home in the atmosphere of a Hellenistic-Christian conceptuality and piety, which is foreign to Paul's description of the redemptive event.[7] It centers on a Christology of appearance (*epiphaneia*, 1 Tim 6:14; 2 Tim 1:10; 4:1, 8)[8] and on a characterization of either God or Christ as "Savior" (*sōter*, 2 Tim 1:10; Titus 3:4-6). In addition, the piety of the *P.E.* is characterized by a host of non-Pauline terms.[9] Further, the pleonastic and flowery language of the *P.E.* heightens its non-Pauline character as seen, for instance, in phrases such as "to live sober, upright and godly" (*sophronos kai dikaios kai eusebos*, Titus 2:12); and "that we may lead a quiet and peaceable life 'with every godliness and seriousness'" (*hina eremon kai hesychion bion diagomen en pasei eusebeiai kai semnoteti*, 1 Tim 2:2).

In other words, when the author blends central concepts of the "original" Paul with his Hellenistic conceptuality, they lose their original meaning and now become worn-out language. For instance, "righteousness" (*dikaiosunē*)—except in 2 Tim 4:8—no longer has its Pauline meaning of God's redemptive intervention in Christ, but instead signifies a pragmatic moral injunction (see "aim at righteousness," 1 Tim 6:11; 2 Tim 2:22); "all scripture... is profitable—for training (*pros paideian*) in righteousness" (2 Tim 3:16; see also Titus 3:5). In fact, the original meaning of Paul's use of the verb *to justify* (*dikaioun*) is only present in texts in which the author incorporates early Christian liturgical traditions in his letters (1 Tim 3:16; Titus 3:7).

In addition, Paul's correlation of the noun *righteousness* and the verb "to justify" (i.e., *dikaio-* terminology) with "faith" (*pistis*), "the law" (*nomos*) and "works" (*erga*) is either absent or possesses different connotation. Kümmel observes: "Frequently 'faith' (*pistis*) continues to indicate the maintenance of the faith (e.g., 1 Tim 1:5) as well as the rule of faith (1 Tim 3:9; 6:10; 2 Tim 4:7), so that often the formula 'in faith' (*en pistei*) appears (1 Tim 1:2; 2:7 and elsewhere) [see note 6, p.131 above]. Indeed, in parallel with this sense of 'faith' [*pistis*] stands 'sound doctrine' [*kale didaskalia*] (1 Tim 4:6). . . . This rationalistic ethical description of Christian existence and the Christian obligation corresponds to the use of the plural 'good works' [*erga agatha*] (as in Eph 2:10), which is stressed in the same way (1 Tim 2:10; Titus 2:14)."[10]

Except for the liturgical piece of Titus 3:4-7, which contrasts "works of righteousness that we had done" (v. 5) with justification by grace (v. 7), the frequent occurrence of "works" (*erga*) in the *P.E.* is always conjoined with the adjectives "good" (*kala* or *agatha*, 1 Tim 2:10; 3:1; 5:10, 22; 6:18; 2 Tim 1:9; 2:21; 3:17; 4:5, 14, 18; Titus 1:16; 2:7, 14; 3:1, 8, 14). Furthermore, "the infrequent use of *en Christō*, which is almost wholly restricted to a combination with abstract nouns in a way that is never encountered in Paul,"[11] coupled with the virtual omission of terms such as *body* (*sōma*) and *Spirit* (*pneuma*) (see 2 Tim 1:14 and Titus 3:5) shows clearly the distance between the Paul of history and the Paul of the *P.E.*

## THE THEOLOGICAL IDENTITY OF THE PASTORAL EPISTLES

We must realize that the religious worldview of the *P.E.* differs radically from that of the Pauline original. The difference is in no small measure due to the author's need to adapt Paul's language and thought to an entirely new historical context. Since the author is not interested in an archaeological search for the original Paul, he understands faithfulness to Paul's gospel to consist in appropriating that gospel to the new situation of his churches so that it can be a word on target for them. In other words, the Pastor does not consider faithfulness to Paul to consist in a literal transposition of Paul's thought, but rather as a search for innovative strategies that permit Paul to speak in a fresh manner. What to many New Testament scholars seems to be "a fall from the true Paul" is for the Pastor an appropriate reinterpretation and reinstatement of Paul's gospel.

This reinterpreted and relevant Paul must safeguard the
continuity of the true Pauline gospel in the church by addressing
two specific dangers that threaten its life: the danger from within, i.e., inner-ecclesial dissent and the danger from without, i.e.,
socioeconomic pressures and political oppression by Roman society and the state.

The danger from without is brought about by the new
situation of the church in history. The church cannot any longer
maintain its sectarian character and remain a contra-society in
the Pauline sense, i.e., a community that is basically opposed to
the world. Since history seems to have a continuing flow, it is
perceived in a way that differs from Paul's perception. For instance, Paul's conviction that "the appointed time has grown
short" (1 Cor 7:29) is no longer a live issue for the church of
the *P.E.* because the church has now an urgent need to secure
a stable position within the structures of the ongoing world of
Roman society.

Thus it must face the issue of how to be *in mundo, sed
non mundi*, i.e., how to adapt itself to its new situation in the
world. Although the Pastor remains committed to the conviction
of Paul and early Christianity that the eschatological judgment
and the ultimate revelation of the glory of God are to be expected
(1 Tim 6:14, 15; 2 Tim 4:8; Titus 2:13), his adoption of a
triumphant *epiphaneia* Christology (see above) and his emphasis
on matters of ecclesial order and administration (1 Tim 2:1-12;
Titus 1:5—2:10) show his fading interest in the imminent coming of the end time. The author actually advocates cautious
accommodation to the secular world of the Roman Empire:
Prayers and intercessions are to be made "for kings and all who
are in high positions that we may lead a quiet and peaceable
life, godly and respectful in every way" (1 Tim 2:1-2).

Moreover, he insists that a bishop must "be well thought
of by outsiders" (1 Tim 3:7), while young widows should "marry,
bear children, rule their households, and give the enemy no
occasion to revile us" (1 Tim 5:14, see Titus 2:5-8). The author
hopes that the church, by conforming to the moral customs of
Roman society, may lead "a quiet and peaceable life" (1 Tim

2:2) and gain a good report from "outsiders" (1 Tim 3:7) and "opponents" alike (Titus 2:8).

The second concern of the author, i.e., the danger from within, is directly related to the danger from without. It is the result of heretical inroads within the church, which threaten its nonoffensive character by the antisocial behavior that they occasion. The confrontation with heresy preoccupies the author so much that it would be appropriate to call the *P.E.* polemical antiheretical letters. In fact, heretics are "the enemy" (1 Tim 5:14) in a double sense: They not only pervert the orthodoxy of the church but are also liable to evoke the hostile attitude of Roman society against persons who upset its civil and moral order.

It is conspicuous how differently Paul and the Pastor define Christian existence. Hans Conzelmann observes:

> This ideal of a peaceful life differs greatly from Paul's understanding of existence, which reflects the many conflicts of his life; one need only compare this passage [1 Tim 2:2] with the description which the apostle gives in 2 Cor 11:23-33 of his life's difficulties and dangers. Paul lives in the tension between this world and God's world: he joyfully affirmed (in 2 Cor 6:4-10) the suffering of this existence as part of citizenship in the other kingdom . . . the Pastor wishes to become part of the world.[12]

And Norbert Brox comments: "We must notice here, in contrast to the Revelation of John, the beginning of Christianity's accommodation to the world."[13]

Although such observations are correct, they do not sufficiently appreciate the sociocultural situation that prompts the theological response of the author. Indeed, Conzelmann tempers his earlier remarks when he writes: "For an historical understanding it is not enough simply to confront this ethical ideal [that of the *P.E.*] with the ethics of Jesus or Paul. It is necessary to consider the changed situation of the church and to interpret the *P.E.* together with contemporary writings (Luke and the

Apostolic Fathers) in the context of a changing conceptual structure . . . change had to follow the reorientation toward a longer
duration of life in the world."[14]

In fact, the author's conception of what life in an ongoing
world demands is directly related to his response to the danger
from within. The church's desire for peace and stability in its
relation to the world matches its desire to eradicate heretical
thought and practice within the church. The author fears that
if the heretical opposition, with its emancipatory asocial behavior
and deviant thought, prevails, the Roman authorities and society
at large will threaten the very survival of the church. Indeed,
the author's opposition to heresy is motivated not only by the
limits that "Paul's" gospel draws between church and world, i.e.
by an over-the-shoulder look at the reaction of Roman society,
but especially by the limits that his gospel draws between orthodoxy and heresy. As Brox correctly observes, "Notwithstanding the overlap with a pragmatic, 'opportune' mentality, the
distinctive character of the Pastoral Epistles is maintained in
two ways: in the vitality and motivation which is grounded in
the preaching of Christ and the boundaries which this understanding of faith [in 2 Timothy] draws in a situation of persecution, since the Pastoral Epistles accomplish and accept a re-
duction to that what is most essential to the Christian
confession."[15]

The author's method of dealing with his opponents makes
it difficult to gain an intelligible profile of the heretics. His desire
to contemporize Paul's authority for his churches directly contradicts Paul's own method of dealing with heretical movements
because, as we saw (see p. 39, above), the delicate balance in
Paul between coherence and contingency is here displaced by a
fixed coherent structure that has no direct relation to the contingent crisis situation which the *P.E.* must face. Instead the
coherence of the gospel functions here to drown the heretical
opposition into a sea of rhetorical attacks, and thus obfuscates
the gospel's real nature. The author demands that church officials
refrain from any contact with heretics because discussions with

them are deemed to be not only dangerous, but even superfluous: "Avoid disputing about words (*logomachein*), which does no good, but only ruins the hearers" (2 Tim 2:14; see also 1 Tim 6:20; 2 Tim 2:33; Titus 3:9). Instead, the proper way to deal with heretics is either "to correct the opponents" (2 Tim 2:24) or "to have nothing to do with godless and silly myths" (1 Tim 4:7). "One can describe the situation in this way: the Pastoral Epistles actually do not combat the heresy, but rather the heretics."[16] The fiction of Pauline authorship becomes here very clear: "Paul" not only warns against the influx of present heresies in the church (1 Tim 1:3, 19-20; 6:20; 2 Tim 2:16; 3:8; Titus 1:10; 3:9), but also predicts these same heresies for the future end time (1 Tim 4:1-5; 2 Tim 3:1f., 13; 4:3f.). Thus Paul's prediction of future heresies and his active struggle with present heresies have identical heresies in mind. Indeed, it is precisely in this way that the author attempts to bridge the gulf separating the time of the historical Paul from that of his Paul.

We conclude, then, that in terms of the situation he must face, the author offers us an impressive portrait of Paul: His Paul not only combats present heresies (1 Tim 1:19-20; 2 Tim 2:17) and not only prophesies heresies to come in the end time (1 Tim 4:1-5), but also gives orders and exhortations to his coworkers concerning how to conduct worship and organize the life of the church. Moreover, Paul is the *sole* apostle, a person who enjoys indisputable authority and whose gospel is the sole norm of Christian truth. And, finally, Paul's words are all the more binding because the author casts them in the form of a farewell address, i.e., as the last will and testament of the apostle, who has suffered for the sake of the gospel and who now from his death cell bids his successors to suffer likewise for the truth of the gospel (2 Tim 1:8; 2:3; 4:5, 17) and to conserve "the deposit" of faith (*parathēkē* 1 Tim 6:20; 2 Tim 1:12, 14) unblemished. In this manner "Paul" ensures the continuity of the tradition amid the discontinuities of history so later generations can render his orthodox gospel faithfully.

# Paul's Legacy in the Book of Acts

There can be no doubt that Paul is the hero of Luke-Acts. One might even be tempted to call Acts the "Acts of Paul" instead of "The Acts of the Apostles."

## THE PORTRAIT OF PAUL

Although we hear about other apostles and missionaries in chapters 1–15, they all disappear rapidly from the scene. James, the brother of John, is killed by Herod Agrippa (12:2). Peter—so prominent along with John in chapters 2–12—disappears suddenly and almost forever in chapter 12: "Then he left and went to another place" (12:17). Stephen, one of the seven Hellenists (6:1-6) is soon martyred (7:55-60), and we never hear again from the other Hellenists, except for Philip, whose missionary activity in Samaria is described by Luke[17] in 8:14-19 (see also 21:8: "we went into the house of Philip the evangelist, one of the seven"). Apart from Barnabas, the prophets and teachers of the Antioch church (13:1-2) are never mentioned again. And even Barnabas, Paul's companion on his missionary journeys, drops out of the picture when he travels to Cyprus after a quarrel with Paul over John Mark (15:37). We do not hear again from James—the brother of the Lord and the president of the Jerusalem church—after his presence at the Apostolic Council (chapter 15) until Paul's last visit to Jerusalem (21:17-26). Moreover, almost no other apostles, missionaries, or disciples receive any attention.

In fact, Paul occupies center stage from chapter 13 on. Luke has introduced him to the reader in the narrative of the stoning of Stephen (7:58–8:1), and subsequently in the stories of his violent persecution of Christians (9:1-2) and of his sudden conversion and call (9:3-19). In fact, in the conversion story the theme appears that will characterize Paul's missionary activity throughout when the risen Lord announces to Ananias: "He is a chosen instrument (*skeuos eklogēs*) of mine, to carry my name before the Gentiles and kings and the sons of Israel; for I will show him how much he must suffer for the sake of my name" (*osa dei auton hypo tou onomatos mou pathein*; 9:15-16). Indeed, from chapter 13 through the end of the book Paul seems to be Luke's exclusive hero. One receives the impression that there were no fellow missionaries besides him, as if Paul alone were responsible for carrying the gospel to the nations and finally to Rome, the heart of the Roman Empire. This impression is reinforced when Luke, in recording the commission of the risen Lord to his disciple-apostles to be his witnesses "to the end of the earth" (1:8), limits this commission in the course of his narrative to Asia Minor, Greece, and finally to Rome, i.e., to the Pauline mission in the west. We hear nothing about a mission to the Jewish Diaspora in Babylonia and East Asia (see Peter's mission to "the circumcision" in Gal 2:7), or about missions to Egypt, North Africa, Illyria, and the Balkan (see Rom 15:20).

However, it is important to understand that notwithstanding the prominence of Peter and Paul in *Acts*, Luke does not intend to thematize his book in terms of *biographical* perspectives. Rather his basic theme is announced in 1:8: "But you will receive power when the Holy Spirit has come upon you; and you will be my witnesses in Jerusalem, in all Judea and Samaria, and to the ends of the earth."

In other words, it seems that Luke is preoccupied with geographical instead of biographical perspectives. However, even the geographical perspective is secondary to Luke's real purpose in Acts: God alone initiates the worldwide mission of the church. Since God's sovereign will and plan determine the mission, it is in no way the initiative and work of human agents, such as Peter or Paul. Luke, then, does not engage in hero worship of Paul. Rather he is an instrument of God's plan of salvation, a chosen instrument (9:15) and a "witness" (22:15), who from the time of his call is totally dependent on the guidance of the Spirit (1:8). For instance, just as the Spirit commands Peter to baptize the Roman centurion Cornelius (11:12, 15), so the Holy Spirit calls Barnabas and Paul to the Gentile mission

(13:2-4); compels Paul to go where he does not want to go (16:6-7); guides his missionary plans (19:21); predicts his forthcoming sufferings (20:23; 21:11-14) and inspires his interpretation of the Scriptures (28:25). In other words, since the mission to the Gentiles is not the fruit of human planning but solely due to God's providential guidance, we may call Luke's essential theme "confusione hominum—Dei providentia" ("where humans fail, God's providence rules").

To be sure, notwithstanding the fact that Paul's role in Acts is that of a chosen instrument (9:15), he is a highly prominent figure: The mission "to the ends of the earth" (1:8) refers unmistakably to him, since he—as we noticed above—almost single-handedly carries the gospel in ever-widening missionary conquests from Antioch to Rome.

However, we must note that Paul's prominence in Acts has nothing to do with Paul as a writer of letters. As John Knox observes, "the Paul of the letters is a great letter writer and a poor speaker (2 Cor 10:10), whereas the Paul of Acts is a great speaker and no letter writer at all."[18] Although scholars continue to debate whether Luke was acquainted with Paul's letters but ignored them or did not know of their existence, the truly important fact is that there are no references to Paul's letters in Acts. In other words, the primary problem that Paul's letters raise, i.e., the problem of the relation of their singularity to their catholicity, is no problem at all for Luke. In fact, in Acts Paul is indeed a great speaker but proclaims an indistinct kerygma. All his speeches are similar, if not parallel, to "the apostolic kerygma" (C. H. Dodd[19]), and especially resemble the speeches of Peter. And so Luke propagates an ecumenical and catholic Paul who always preaches the same message wherever he goes and who faithfully adheres to the kerygma that is authorized by the Jerusalem church (chapter 15).

Thus Luke solves the problem of the relation between singularity and catholicity in Paul's letters by minimizing the distinctiveness of Paul's thought. In fact, the relation between the apostle and his thought is here decided in favor of personal apostolic greatness. What evokes admiration is not the distinctiveness of Paul's message, but rather the remarkable career and missionary success of this supreme witness of Christ. The parallelism between Peter and Paul in Acts actually contributes to Luke's portrait of a catholic Paul. Paul resembles Peter, the most prominent apostle in chapters 2–12 and an important leader of the apostolic college (15:7-11) in every way. Thus Luke reports a series of almost identical acts and experiences of both of them: healing-miracles (3:2-3; 14:8-9); raisings from the dead (9:40-41; 20:10); exorcisms (5:16; 16:16); miraculous escapes from prison (5:17-18; 12:2-17; 16:23-24), and confrontations with magicians (8:14-24; 19:13-17). Even their speeches seem to be equal in number (about nine speeches). Moreover, both of them are devoted to the unity of the church and are obedient to the dictates of the apostolic college (15:14-20; 21:15-26).

And yet the parallelism between Peter and Paul breaks down at a crucial point: Peter is an apostle, whereas Paul is not. Luke seems to contradict himself here. How is it possible that Paul—the most important witness to Christ, the one who occupies Luke's exclusive attention in chapters 13–28 and the one whose witness in the capital of the Roman Empire forms the climax of the book—is not accorded the title "apostle," a title upon which the historical Paul insisted and for which he regularly fought in his letters?

However, Luke has even his Paul admit that he does not qualify as an apostle. Thus he says in his Antioch speech: "But God raised him (Jesus) from the dead; and for many days he appeared to those who came up with him from Galilee to Jerusalem, and they are now his witnesses to the people" (13:30-31). Indeed, Peter confirms that latecomers such as Paul cannot be numbered among the apostles: "God raised him on the third day and allowed him to appear, not to all the people but to us who were chosen by God as witnesses, and who ate and drank with him after he rose from the dead" (10:40-41). It is peculiar indeed that Paul, the foremost witness to Christ among the Gentiles (22:15, 21), does not qualify as an apostle, especially when we remember that he is God's chosen instrument (9:15), appointed by God to be his witness "to all the world of what you have seen and heard" (22:15); and the one to whom Christ gave a special commission: "I have appeared to you for this purpose, to appoint you to serve and testify to the things in which you have seen me and to those in which I will appear to you" (26:16-17).

This apparent contradiction is not a deliberate move on Luke's part to downplay Paul's importance or to make him a submissive servant of the Jerusalem apostles. Rather, Luke wants to sketch Paul as a pillar of orthodoxy, as the one who upholds the truth of the common apostolic kerygma upon which the unity of the church is based. In other words, what is at stake for Luke is "the basic solidity" ("la soliditá," *La Sainte Bible,* Paris, 1956; *asphaleia,* Luke 1:4) of the gospel message, which requires a firm historical foundation. And this dictates that admission to apostleship must fulfill two basic criteria: one must have been a witness to Jesus' life and work, and a witness to his bodily resurrection and ascension (1:3-9).

Another feature of Luke's portrait of Paul is the ambivalent and contradictory manner in which he describes Paul's suffering. Notwithstanding his emphasis on Paul as the suffering witness (9:15-16, see p. 49, above), Paul's missionary activity seems to be a success story in the Hellenistic manner of extolling great men. Indeed, wherever Paul goes, crowds gather, cities turn out, and civic problems are engendered.

For instance, Jews in Thessalonica cry: "These people who have been turning the world (*tēn oikoumenēn*) upside down have come here also, . . . [and] they are all acting contrary to the decrees of the emperor, saying that there is another king, named Jesus" (17:6-7). And Paul's preaching in the hall of Tyrannus is reported as follows: "This [preaching] continued for two years, so that all the residents of Asia, both Jews and Greeks, heard the word of the Lord" (19:10). Moreover, Demetrius, the silversmith, warns: "Not only at Ephesus but in almost the whole of Asia this Paul has persuaded and drawn away a considerable number of people (*hikanon ochlon*) by saying that gods made with hands are not gods. And there is danger not only that this trade of ours may come into disrepute but also that the temple of the great goddess Artemis will be scorned, and she will be deprived of her majesty that brought all Asia and the world to worship her" (19:26-27).

And even when things get rough, Paul finds immediate comfort. For instance, amid severe Jewish heckling God tells Paul in a vision in Corinth: "Do not be afraid, but speak and do not be silent; for I am with you, and no one will lay a hand on you to harm you (*tou kakōsai se*), for there are many in the city who are my people (*laos polus*)" (18:9-10). A similar scenario occurs in Philippi where prison doors open, the jailer is converted, the magistrates apologize to Paul and Silas, and escort them out of the city (16:25-40).

Luke, then, describes Paul frequently as the exact opposite of his self-description in 2 Corinthians 10–13. In Acts he is not the apostle of weakness who confesses "whenever I am weak, then I am strong" (2 Cor 12:10), but rather a person of obvious strength and glamor. Indeed, it is ironic that the Paul of Acts resembles in many ways those self-serving apostles whom the historical Paul curses as false apostles in 2 Corinthians. In fact, Luke often portrays Paul as a "divine man" (*theios anēr*) who incarnates the epiphany of God in this world; a man of wisdom and eloquence; a man who performs healings, exorcises evil spirits, and does other "extraordinary miracles . . . so that when the handkerchiefs or aprons that had touched his skin were brought to the sick, their diseases left them, and the evil spirits came out of them" (19:11-12; see also 16:17-18). The natives of Malta even proclaim Paul to be "a god" (*theon*), after he casually shakes a poisonous viper into the fire (28:1-6).

Paul also enjoys the favor of the powerful of this world and impresses them with his eloquence: he converts proconsuls (13:12: Sergius Paulus on Cyprus), is an honored guest at the villa of the governor of Malta (28:7: Publius), impresses procurators and kings such as Felix, Festus, and Agrippa (26:30-32), is saved by the tribune after a riot in Jerusalem (23:22), and again by a Roman centurion after a shipwreck (27:43).

However, we must note that Luke's portrait of Paul is
not simply the product of a theology of glory. Although scholars
have frequently contrasted Paul's theology of the cross with
Luke's portrayal of Christ and have charged Luke with a theology
of glory,[20] these charges betray a misunderstanding of Luke's
intent. Even though a theology of the cross is alien to Luke, he
develops his own theology of suffering.

In the first place, we have seen that Luke emphasizes the
theme of suffering in Paul's call (9:16). Secondly, the final part
of Paul's career (see 19:21–28:31) is portrayed as a *via dolorosa*.
Roloff comments that these final chapters constitute "the climax
of Luke's portrait of Paul and thus the climax of the book as a
whole. The theme of this main part is the road of Paul from
Jerusalem to Rome. [The verse] 19:21 is the point of reversal
and at the same time the solemn introduction of this part."[21]
Indeed, 19:21 in Acts resembles in importance the text that
signals the turning point in the Gospel of Luke. Just as in Luke
9:51 Jesus' passion and resurrection are adumbrated in the
words: "When the days drew near for him (Jesus) to be taken
up, he set his face to go to Jerusalem," so the turning point in
Acts' narrative of Paul is sounded in 19:21: "Now after these
things had been accomplished, Paul resolved in the Spirit to go
through Macedonia and Achaia, and then to go on to Jerusalem.
He said, 'After I have gone there, I must also see Rome' " (*dei
me kai Romēn idein*). The *dei*- clause ("must") in 19:21 points
to God's sovereign providence and is reiterated in 23:11: "Keep
up your courage! For just as you have testified for me in Jerusalem, so you must bear witness also in Rome" (*houtō se dei
kai eis Romen martyrēsai*). Indeed, in 19:21 Rome is mentioned
for the first time in Acts as the goal and climax of Paul's witness
(see also 23:11). And this foreordained plan of God opens up
dramatically Paul's *via dolorosa*, for Paul's way to Jerusalem and
Rome is marked by suffering.

Another reference to Luke's gospel is instructive here.
The "must" clause of Acts 19:21 and 23:11 recalls clearly the
"must" of Jesus' suffering in Luke's Gospel: "The Son of man
must (*dei*) suffer many things, and be rejected by the elders and

chief priests and scribes, and be killed" (9:22; see also Luke 17:25; 24:7-26). Indeed, the parallel between Jesus and Paul is striking in Luke's two-volume work. In his gospel Jesus is portrayed as the supreme martyr who, like a Socrates figure, is unjustly convicted and murdered on the cross. The death of Jesus is an immoral act of the Jews against a supremely moral person, a fact to which the Roman centurion at the foot of the cross gives witness: "Certainly this man was innocent" (*dikaios*, Luke 23:47). Just as Luke in his Gospel describes Jesus' journey to Jerusalem as his *via dolorosa* and passion (9:51; 19:28), which climaxes in his death (23:46), so he portrays Paul in Acts as the one who is the innocent victim of false Jewish charges (26:31-32) and who now travels the road of suffering from Jerusalem to Rome, where death awaits him. Like the master, so the disciple! Just as Jesus fulfills the role of the suffering Mosaic prophet (Acts 2:23; 3:18-26; 7:51-52), so do his witnesses—Stephen, John, Peter, and especially Paul.

For instance, after Paul's resolve to go to Jerusalem and Rome, there is a plot by the Jews in Greece to kill him, so Paul must change his itinerary (20:3). What follows is Paul's farewell speech to the Ephesian elders in Miletus, which is permeated by the theme of suffering: "And now, as a captive to the Spirit, I am on my way to Jerusalem, not knowing what will happen to me there, except that the Holy Spirit testifies to me in every city that imprisonment and persecutions are waiting for me (*desma kai thlipseis*). But I do not count my life of any value to myself, if only I may finish my course (*ton dromon mou*; see 2 Tim 4:7) and the ministry (*tēn diakonian*; see 1 Tim 1:12) that I received from the Lord Jesus, to testify to the good news of God's grace" (20:22-24).

The curious fact that Luke does not report Paul's death in Rome in the final chapter of Acts (chapter 28) is actually not surprising because it agrees with his overall plan to sketch the victorious march of the gospel from Jerusalem to Rome (1:8). It does not mean that Luke is ignorant about Paul's death, since he has prepared us for it in the farewell scenes of the previous chapters.

From chapter 20 on, warnings of suffering, captivity, and death come regularly. For example, disciples in Tyre (21:4) and the prophet Agabus in Caesarea (21:10-12) beg him not to go to Jerusalem. Paul, however, rejects these warnings: "What are you doing, weeping and breaking my heart? For I am ready not only to be bound, but even to die in Jerusalem (*apothanein eis Jerusalēm*) for the name of the Lord Jesus" (21:13).

Indeed, the theme of Paul's suffering and imminent death has been sounded before in chapter 20. The foreboding words "none of you . . . will ever see my face again" (20:25) are followed by a farewell scene at the harbor, which is marked by tears, sorrow, and embraces (20:38). We must notice that the theme of suffering is properly placed at the end of Paul's farewell speech in Miletus (20:18-35) because it signifies Paul's last will and testament and, moreover, informs the reader of Paul's imminent death in Rome. Thus the speech is quite similar to the composition of 2 Timothy in adopting the genre of a farewell speech, i.e., Paul's last will and testament prior to his death (see 2 Tim 4:6-18).

And so Luke brings his book to a climax with a picture of Paul who, even in prison, proclaims the gospel in Rome "with all boldness and without hindrance" (28:31).

We see then that Luke develops an important theology of suffering, characterized by the theme "from suffering to glory." Indeed, suffering is not only the necessary prelude to glory, but also the foil for this-worldly triumph. Whereas the historical Paul emphasizes a hidden glory in suffering, which the world cannot perceive (2 Cor 12:10) but which is nevertheless a proleptic sign of the end of all suffering in the coming apocalyptic glory of God (Rom 8:18), Luke underscores a different emphasis: Suffering is a prelude not only to eschatological glory (14:22), but also to this-worldly triumph and glory.

Thus in Acts Paul's *via dolorosa* from Jerusalem to Rome is guided by God's providence in such a way that God secures Paul's safety over and again and enables him to preach the gospel in the capital of the Roman Empire "with all boldness and without hindrance" (28:31). In fact, Luke nowhere provides an answer to the question why innocent people must suffer in this world; his only answer is the dogmatic assertion "it was/is necessary" (*dei*, Luke 24:7, 26, 44; Acts 9:16; 14:22; 17:3; 19:21; 23:11; 27:24; see above), an assertion which is buttressed by an appeal to the Old Testament Scriptures.

We should be aware that a significant shift occurs in Paul's portrait in 19:21–28:31. The picture of Paul the missionary now changes to that of Paul the accused. After Paul, the bold evangelist, has given his last missionary speech to the elders of Miletus in Ephesus (20:18-35), he suddenly becomes Paul on trial, who must defend himself against the charge of apostasy from Judaism (21:20-25; 22:3-21; 23:6-10; 24:10-21; 25:8, 10; 26:1-23). In other words, Paul is redesigned as the faithful Jew in these chapters.

Far from rejecting the law and circumcision, he observes the Torah and its ritual demands (21:21-27): He circumcises Timothy (16:3), announces that he is still a Pharisee (23:6), and believes "everything laid down according to the law or written in the prophets" (24:14; see 26:4-8). Moreover, he represents the best in Jewish religion, the "hope in the promise made by God to our ancestors" (26:6), i.e., "the resurrection of the dead" (23:6; 24:21; 26:23). In this manner Luke's Paul demonstrates the emptiness of the charges leveled against him as described by the elders and James: "You see, brother, how many thousands of believers there are among the Jews, and they are all zealous for the law. They have been told about you that you teach all the Jews living among the Gentiles to forsake Moses, and that you tell them not to circumcise their children or observe the customs" (21:20-21).[22] Paul complies with their request to prove such charges false by going to the temple to purify himself along with four men who have taken a vow (21:22-26); in this way "all will know" that Paul himself lives in observance of the law (21:24).

## THE THEOLOGICAL IDENTITY OF ACTS

This sketch of Luke's portrait of Paul must be seen in the context of the overall purpose of his two-volume work. Robert

Tannehill correctly points to the narrative unity of Luke-Acts:
"Change and development are expected in such a narrative, yet
unity is maintained because the scenes and characters contribute
to a larger story that determines the significance of each part. . . .
Luke-Acts is a unified narrative because the chief human characters (John the Baptist, Jesus, the apostles, Paul) share in a
mission which expresses a single controlling purpose—the purpose of God."[23]

Indeed, Luke highlights God's purpose in his narrative
by frequently using the phrases "the purpose of God" (*boulē
tou theou*) and "it was/is necessary" (*dei*).[24] These phrases are
key terms in Luke's conception of salvation history, which moves
from Israel via the ministry of Jesus to the church of the Gentiles;
Luke's purpose is "to write an orderly account . . . so that you
may know the truth concerning the things about which you have
been instructed" (Luke 1:3-4).

Luke's narrative, dominated by the plan of God as a single
controlling purpose (see Tannehill), unfolds its salvation-his-
torical theme in terms of three interrelated subthemes: (1) the
theme of the unity of the church, which also prompts Luke's
antiheretical stance; (2) the theme of the political legitimacy of
the church, which motivates Luke's pro-Roman attitude; and
(3) the theme of the theological legitimacy of the church, which
stresses the continuity between the church and Israel. All these
themes are designed to meet the problems that Luke's church
faces at the end of the first century A.D.

The first theme portrays the church of the apostolic past
as the *Una Sancta Apostolica*, which in its unity, harmony, and
peace provides the model for Luke's own church. This idealized
picture of the apostolic beginnings of the church, which is a
mixture of historical memory and Luke's own literary purpose,
emphasizes the purity and unity of the beginnings of the church
and thus gives Luke a powerful weapon against heretics. For
instance, Paul's farewell address to the elders of Ephesus in
Miletus has a specific antiheretical focus: "Keep watch over
yourselves and over all the flock, of which the Holy Spirit has
made you overseers (*episkopous*), to shepherd the church of

God that he obtained with the blood of his own Son (*tou idiou*). I know that after I have gone (*meta tēn aphixin mou*), savage wolves will come in among you, not sparing the flock. Some even from your own group will come distorting the truth (*lalountes diestrammena*) in order to entice the disciples to follow them. Therefore be alert (*dio grēgoreite*), remembering that for three years I did not cease night or day to warn everyone with tears" (20:28-31).

Here Paul contemplates the future and addresses the danger Luke's church faces in the here and now. The heretical danger is twofold: There is a threat not only from "savage wolves" (v. 29) who will invade the church from the outside, but also from heretics who will arise within the church with their claim to present the gospel in a truer and more effective fashion.

And so Luke combats them by stressing the public, nonsecretive character of Paul's gospel (20:20) and his proclamation of "the whole purpose of God" (20:27). Although there are only few references in Acts to the present threat of heresy (8:9-24; 20:28-31),[25] Paul's farewell address in 20:17-35 demonstrates that Luke's antiheretical stance underscores not only the theme of the unity of the church, but also the theme of the continuity of tradition. Therefore "Paul" emphasizes that the overseers ([*episkopoi*] v. 28, who are identical with the elders [*presbyteroi*] of v. 17) are charged with the leadership of Luke's church and must guard the continuity between past and present, i.e., between Paul's gospel and the present church.

The fact that Luke frames this speech of Paul as a farewell address underscores its importance because it carries all the weight of a last will and testament. In this context Roloff observes:

> The *Sitz im Leben* of the farewell discourse is the historical location of the institution or group, reflecting on the heritage which has been entrusted to it. The focus of interest is not so much the personal fate of the central figure of the past, but the historical effect of his work. The later generation begins to understand its own historical location

when it realizes how much it has been shaped by its past heritage and is able to preserve this heritage for its own future.[26]

In short, the genre of the farewell discourse occupies an important function when historical continuity has become a problem, which in Luke's case means the continuity of the tradition from the second to the third Christian generation. Indeed, Paul's farewell address occupies a unique place among the speeches of Acts: It is the only speech of Paul that is addressed to Christians and the only speech that is not a response to a specific urgent local problem.

Moreover, it is the only speech in which the person of Paul himself is the focus and in which he presents to the church a synopsis of past, present, and future issues. Thus the speech emphasizes the continuity of tradition in the face of disruptive heresies.

The second theme, which runs like a red thread through Acts, deals with the political legitimacy of the church. Luke's positive attitude toward the Roman Empire and its officials is remarkable, especially when it is compared with the radical stance of the Revelation to John against imperial Rome or with the more cautious disposition of the Pastoral Epistles. Indeed, Luke marks the beginning of the apologetic literature, which will flower in the second century A.D. For instance, Justin Martyr claims that Christians are the emperor's best allies in the cause of peace and good order (Apol. 1., 11:1–12:1), while Tertullian posits Christianity as the soul of the empire (Apol. 1. 25–33). Although Luke has a much more cautious attitude to the state than the Apologists and, moreover, addresses Christians and not Roman emperors, he intimates that when Christians behave properly they have nothing to fear from the state. The extent to which Luke articulates the political inoffensiveness of Christianity and its favorable reception by Roman officials is indeed surprising.

Just as the procurator Pilate pronounces Jesus innocent (and that three times, Luke 23:4, 14, 22), so the procurator

Festus and King Agrippa declare Paul innocent of the charges of the Jews (26:32; see also 23:9; 24:16, 20; 25:8, 11, 25). Moreover, the proconsul of Achaia, Gallio, refuses to hear Jewish accusations against Paul (18:12-15), and, as noticed above (see p. 53, above), a Roman centurion and tribunes guarantee Paul's safety during a riot in Jerusalem (21:27-36; 23:22) while another Roman centurion does not allow his soldiers to kill Paul during a shipwreck off Malta (27:43).

The favorable reaction of Roman officials to Paul is all the more surprising in the face of the continuous and politically effective accusations of the Jews: "These people [Paul and Silas] who have been turning the world upside down have come here also. . . . They are all acting contrary to the decrees of the emperor, saying that there is another king named Jesus" (17:6-7; cf. 16:21). Luke, like the apologists in the second century A.D., attempts with these pro-Roman features of his narrative to discredit the Roman charge of the subversive and revolutionary character of Christianity. Indeed, we must not forget that, in Luke's time, slander, ostracism, and the threat of persecution by Roman society were very real. And these dangers were all the more acute because the church was considered to be no longer a Jewish sect, but an independent movement (the term *Christianos* occurs in the New Testament only three times— twice in Acts [11:26; 28:28] and once in 1 Peter [4:16]). In other words, Christians have now become a *tertium genus,* "a third race," and outsiders call them "Christians" instead of Jews (11:26). And this means that the protection Judaism enjoyed as a *religio licita* (a protected religion under Roman law) is no longer theirs. Christians are now in danger of being outlawed as a *superstitio nova ac malefica,* a term used by Roman law to condemn new Oriental cults. Luke's pro-Roman attitude, then, is motivated by his attempt to protect the church against the threats of persecution, illegality and social ostracism by the Roman state. In fact, this may well be one reason why Luke chooses not to narrate Paul's death at the hands of the Romans (see p. 55, above).[27]

Luke's third theme focuses on the theological legitimacy of the church, which preoccupies him probably more deeply than the other themes. Although this issue is directly related to those of the unity of the church and of its political legitimacy, Luke's basic problem concerns the theological status of Christianity as a "third race" (*tertium genus*). For what will the status of this "third race" be now that it is no longer a part of either Judaism or pagan society?[28] This problem has become all the more acute for the many recent Gentile converts to Christianity, who as "God fearers" (*phoboumenoi*; *sebomenoi*) were formerly associated with the synagogue. For what does constitute henceforth their religious identity?

In other words, how can the church claim a legitimate identity when it professes a Jewish messiah as its Lord while the Jews themselves explicitly reject this "Christian" messiah? And how can the church claim to be "the true Israel" of God (see, Luke 24:44) when it breaks down the very heart of Judaism, i.e., the covenant, the Torah, and circumcision? How can the church appropriate for itself the promises of the Jewish Scriptures and claim to represent in Christ the fulfillment of God's covenant with Abraham when it has ostensibly separated itself from its parent religion by ceasing to be obedient to Israel's Torah? Moreover, this situation was exacerbated by the fact that the church had practically no success in converting Jews, notwithstanding its claims that the gospel primarily applies to them (2:38-42; see the emphasis on "first to you (Jews)" [3:26; 13:46]).

And if Christianity is no longer committed to the Torah and to its Jewish heritage, how can it dismiss the Roman charge that it is simply another new mystery religion—a charge which, for instance, the Athenians level against Paul: "He [Paul] seems to be a proclaimer of foreign divinities (*xenōn daimoniōn*)"; "May we know what this new teaching is (*kainē didachē*) that you are presenting?" (17:18-19).

Luke now addresses the issue of the church's theological legitimacy by emphasizing the continuity of the church with Israel, i.e., the continuity of God's salvation-history. Therefore, his long section on "the trial of Paul" (chapters 21–28) intends to demonstrate that Christianity is the fulfillment of Judaism rather than its abrogation. And so Luke points out that, whereas the rejection of the gospel by the Jews must be attributed to their ignorance and evil stubbornness (28:26-27), Paul himself stands squarely within the Jewish tradition. In fact, these immoral Jewish traits have also led them to crucify their own Messiah, Jesus (2:40; 3:17; 13:27; 17:30; see Luke 23:34). Therefore the church is not a new mystery religion or a new philosophical sect (17:21), but instead constitutes the true people of God, i.e., the true Israel.

## SUMMARY

Paul's portrait in Acts, then, must be seen within the larger context of Luke's overall purpose. First of all, Luke portrays Paul as the great ecumenical catholic missionary who plays a crucial role in the worldwide purpose of God. Indeed, the mandate of the risen Lord that all his apostles must be his witnesses "to the ends of the earth ([heōs eschatou tēs gēs]," 1:8) climaxes in God's mandate to Paul: "I have set you to be a light for the Gentiles, so that you may bring salvation to the ends of the earth ([heōs eschatou tēs gēs]," 13:47). In other words, although Luke underscores the cooperative character of the worldwide mission by all the apostles (Luke 24:47; Acts 1:8) and thus the unity of the church's kerygma, it is actually Paul who single-handedly fulfills God's mandate because it is he who brings the gospel to the ends of the earth, i.e., to Rome, the capital of the Roman Empire (28:14-31).

Secondly, Luke's Paul is the one who has always been faithful to the best traditions of Judaism and whose gospel fulfills what Judaism has been hoping for (see p. 57, above).

Thirdly, Luke's Paul is a loyal Roman citizen ([Romaios] 22:25-29; 23:27) who has received protection under Roman law and has demonstrated his political innocence, while at the same time he has received favorable treatment from Roman magistrates.

And finally, Paul's gospel message is in complete harmony with all the "apostolic" witnesses to Jesus. Although Paul cannot be numbered among the apostles, he is nevertheless Christ's greatest witness and in every way obedient to the authority of the Jerusalem church.

Luke's transmission of Pauline tradition, then, takes a peculiar form. Since Luke ignores Paul's letters and uses Paul's terminology only occasionally (see 13:39; 20:28), Pauline tradition in Acts is not based on Paul's literary legacy but is rather a mixture of oral reports, memories, and legends about Paul. In this manner, Luke attempts to integrate Paul into his own ideal image of the church: Paul is the successful missionary who spent all his energy in safeguarding the continuity of the apostolic tradition by maintaining the original harmonious unity of the apostolic beginnings of the church.

## Paul's Legacy in Colossians and Ephesians

Paul's portraits in Colossians and Ephesians have as much in common with each other as they differ from the portraits sketched in the *P.E.* and Acts. Moreover, we must be aware that Colossians and Ephesians are much closer to the thought of the historical Paul than either the *P.E.* or Acts.

Both letters attempt to retain Paul's interpretive method of interweaving coherence and contingency; both refuse to domesticate Paul (in the manner of the *P.E.*) or to present him as a friend of Rome (in the manner of Acts). Furthermore, both these writers are much more indebted to Paul's letters than to Pauline legend. For instance, they both embrace the basic outline and structure of the Pauline letter (see p. 69, below).

It also must be noted that both Colossians and Ephesians emphasize not only the exclusivity of Paul's apostolate, but also the specificity and uniqueness of his gospel. Thus, although they resemble the *P.E.* in highlighting the exclusivity of Paul's apostolate, their perception of Paul's theological stature is radically different (see pp. 67 and 71, below). Therefore, it is not surprising that many scholars consider these letters to be authentically Pauline based on their considerable resemblance to Paul's letters.

## THE THEOLOGY OF COLOSSIANS

Colossians portrays Paul as the theologian of cosmic wisdom. He is the one to whom God has revealed "the mystery that has been hidden throughout the ages and generations but has now been revealed to his saints" (1:26). He is the unique apostle through whom God has made known "the riches of the glory of this mystery, which is Christ among you, the hope of glory" (1:27; author's translation). The author interprets this cosmic wisdom in a strictly christocentric manner and heightens its importance by using a rich wisdom vocabulary. Indeed, the letter is filled with terms such as "wisdom" (*sophia*, 1:9, 28; 2:3, 23; 3:16; 4:5); "knowledge" (*epignosis*, 1:9, 10; 2:2; 3:10); *gnosis*, 2:3); "philosophy" (*philosophia*, 2:8); "perfection" and "perfect" or "mature" (*teleiotes/teleios*, 3:14/1:28; 4:12); and "insight" (*synesis*, 1:9; 2:12). Moreover, he employs verbs that are directly related to the vocabulary of wisdom, such as "to be filled," "to make full" (*pleroō*, 1:9, 25; 2:10; 4:17); "to be fully assured" (*plerophoreō*, 4:12); see also the related nouns "fullness" (*pleroma*, 1:19; 2:9) and "assurance" (*plerophoria*, 2:2).

The wisdom-flavor of these terms is especially evident in phrases such as "Christ himself, in whom are hidden all the treasures of wisdom and knowledge" (*hoi thesauroi tēs sophiās kai gnoseōs*, 2:3) and in the frequent occurrence of the term "mystery" (*mysterion*, 1:26, 27; 2:2; 4:3). Equally noticeable is the recurrent term "all" (*pas*; *panta*), which encompasses not only the cosmic-universal range of the gospel (1:16[2x], 17[2x]; 2:3, 9-10, 19; 3:11), but also the all-encompassing embrace of its ethical demand.[29]

However, the author's accentuation of Christ as cosmic Lord and his rich use of wisdom language do not mean that he has a special propensity for philosophical speculation. To the contrary, he is compelled to use this wisdom-conceptuality because he must confront gnosticizing (Jewish) Christians, who propagate their own theology of wisdom by means of cosmic speculations that are conjoined to cultic practices. These Christians find it necessary to supplement Paul's gospel with a "fuller" gospel. And the cornerstone of this "fuller" gospel is a dualistic cosmology, which—enriched by Jewish-syncretistic elements— proclaims that redemption indeed depends on the work of Christ but not on the work of Christ alone. It depends as well on finding ways to protect Christians against the ruling powers of this fallen universe who exercise their power by preventing Christians from ascending to God's heaven, i.e., from reaching the divine "fullness" (2:3, 9-10, 17).

Therefore, the central theme and argument of the letter are directly related to the author's polemic against this "supplementary" Christology. He introduces a cosmic hymn in 1:15-20, which was a part of the liturgy of the Colossian church, and proceeds to highlight its basic content: It is indeed Christ alone who represents "all the fullness of God" (1:19), "for in him all things in heaven and on earth were created, things visible and invisible, whether thrones or dominions or rulers or powers— all things have been created through him and for him" (1:16). It is Christ alone who is the all-sufficient redeemer; and it is Christ alone whom God has appointed "to reconcile to himself all things, whether on earth or in heaven" (1:20a). But at this point the author underscores his Pauline interpretation of the hymn by inserting that all this has been accomplished by "the blood of his cross" (1:20b). Indeed, on the cross of Christ "[God] disarmed the rulers and authorities and made a public example of them, triumphing over them in him" (2:15; author's translation). And it is this Christ, the author emphasizes, "in whom are hidden all the treasures of wisdom and knowledge" (2:3). However, the author's indebtedness to Paul is not limited to christological matters. The ethical pragmatism of the letter is equally Pauline, and covers the long section of 3:1–4:6. An innovative feature of this section is found in the so-called household codes (3:18–4:1), which appear here for the first time in Christian literature. In fact, ethical exhortation permeates the letter throughout, marked by the verb "to teach" (*didaskō,* 1:28; 2:7; 3:16), a verb Paul rarely uses.

In other words, the author's propensity to use wisdom language actually serves a practical moral purpose. His image for the church is epitomized in these words: "This is the Christ we proclaim, this is the wisdom [*sophia*] in which we thoroughly train everyone and instruct everyone, to make them all perfect [*teleios*] in Christ" (1:28, JB).

The author's antiheretical polemic, then, is undergirded by this practical wisdom. It must remind the Colossian Christians of the radical contrast between the "once" of their pagan life and the "now" of God's redemptive act in Christ (1:21-22, 26). Indeed, their new status in Christ prepares them for the "now" of their new moral task (3:8; see also Eph 2:13; 3:5, 10; esp. Eph 5:8: "For once you were darkness, but now in the Lord you are light. Live as children of light").

Although, as we have seen, the author feels compelled to use wisdom categories in his polemic with heretical Christians, there are probably other reasons as well for his interest in wisdom. He probably was a member of a Pauline school, which after the death of the apostle was founded in Ephesus to appropriate Paul's legacy and transmit it to new generations of Christians. Conzelmann surmises that this Pauline school developed Paul's teaching in the direction of a wisdom theology, which was especially appropriate for Christian witness in the Hellenistic-Gentile world.[30] Moreover, such a leaning toward a wisdom theology actually could point to Paul's own creativity because he himself had initiated a similar move in his first letter to the Corinthians (1 Cor 2:6-16; 10:1-13).

## THE PORTRAIT OF PAUL IN COLOSSIANS

Paul's portrait in Colossians conforms to the overall theological perspective of the letter. Paul is cast as the universal-ecumenical theologian of wisdom who has been granted a special privilege by God to proclaim "the mystery that has been hidden throughout the ages and generations" (1:26), which means "Christ among you, the hope of glory" (1:27; author's translation). Moreover, the picture of Paul as the only authoritative and ideal apostle is enlarged and deepened by emphasizing his "sufferings" (*pathēmata*, 1:24) and his "weary and hard struggle" (*kopiō*; *agonizomai*, 1:29 [JB], and "striving" *agōn*, 2:1). These sufferings and hardships vividly illustrate his complete dedication to the Gentile mission (4:3-4).

Indeed, Paul is the sole apostle: No other apostles are mentioned, and Timothy, Paul's coworker and "our brother" (1:1), is never mentioned again, not even in the long list of greetings (4:10-14—taken over by the author from Philemon 24). Indeed, Paul the exclusive apostle is also Paul the universal-ecumenical apostle: He has preached the gospel "to *every* creature (*en pasei ktisei*) under heaven," (1:23); his gospel "is bearing fruit and growing in the whole world" (*en panti toi kosmoi*, 1:6), and Paul is "warning everyone (*panta anthrōpon*) and teaching everyone (*panta anthrōpon*) in all wisdom, so that we may present everyone (*panta anthrōpon*) mature in Christ" (1:28). Moreover, the sole subject of Paul's preaching is Christ. Paul's portrait in Colossians, then, has one basic theme: the *solus apostolus* who proclaims the *solus Christus*.

We must be aware of the role that memory plays in this exalted view of Paul. The letters are addressed to churches that never had any direct contact with Paul (2:1-5) and were in fact founded by his coworker Epaphras (1:7). Indeed, Colossians presents a Paul "of blessed memory," who has been given a heroic status and who is remembered in these Pauline churches not only as the *solus apostolus*, but also as the martyr whose sufferings (1:24) and constant struggle (1:29; 2:1) for the sake of the church culminated in his imprisonment (4:3; cf. 4:10) and martyrdom (4:18).[31]

## THE THEOLOGY OF EPHESIANS

The close literary dependence of Ephesians on Colossians reflects itself in the many theological similarities between the two letters. Nevertheless, Ephesians is not slavishly dependent on its predecessor but develops its own literary style and theological focus.

To be sure, the structure of the two letters is similar and conforms closely to that of Paul's letters. Moreover, they imitate Paul as well in placing the paraenetic sections after the theological expositions (Col 1–2; 3–4; Eph 1–3; 4–6). However, their purpose and theological perspective show remarkable differences. Whereas Colossians is a personal and contingent letter that addresses specific churches in the Lycus valley and combats a contingent heretical opposition, Ephesians, to the contrary, lacks such personal and contingent features. It is instead an encyclical letter that addresses a group of churches, probably located in Asia Minor, to instruct them in basic matters of theology and ethics.

In fact, the differences between Colossians and Ephesians resemble in many ways the differences between Paul's letters to the Galatians and to the Romans. Both Colossians and Galatians are marked by a close interrelation between coherent theological structure and contingent situation, whereas in Ephesians and Romans the coherent theological structure is so prominent that its relation to contingent situations is either absent (Ephesians) or difficult to determine (Romans).

Therefore, it is not surprising when New Testament interpreters call Romans "a compendium of Christian doctrine" (Melanchthon), "a letter-essay" (Karl Donfried)[32], or "a comprehensive and systematic treatise" (John Lightfoot)[33], or when they characterize Ephesians as "the quintessence of Paulinism" (F. F. Bruce)[34] or as "the spiritual testament of Paul to the church" (Jack T. Sanders).[35]

And in addition to this structural dissimilarity between Ephesians and Colossians, the manner in which Ephesians interprets "the mystery" of revelation is strikingly different from its interpretation in Colossians. This is all the more remarkable because both letters share a "revelation scheme," which is characterized by the contrast between the "once" of the hidden mystery and the "now" of its disclosure in Christ (3:5, 10; cf. Col 1:26).

Whereas the author of Colossians defines the content of the mystery always as Christ (1:26-27; 2:2; see 4:3: "the mystery of Christ"), the author of Ephesians emphasizes its ecclesiological aspect, since here the focus of the mystery (3:3-4; 6:15) is the power of the gospel to unite Jew and Gentile in the one body of Christ (2:14-22; 3:6; 4:15-16). Indeed, ecclesiology dominates the letter throughout. The eulogy at the beginning of the letter (1:3-14) praises the God who "chose us in Christ before the foundation of the world," and determined "as a plan for the fullness of time, to gather up all things in him (Christ), things in heaven and things on earth" (1:4, 10). The God who "is able to accomplish abundantly far more than all we can ask or imagine" (3:20) has now "made him [Christ] the head over all things for the church, which is his body, the fullness of him who fills all in all" (1:22-23).

Indeed, the plan of God, which climaxes in the unity of Jew and Gentile in the one "household of God" (2:19; see 2:11-21), has a cosmic range. It is through the church that "the wisdom of God in its rich variety might now be made known to the rulers and authorities in the heavenly places" (3:10; see 1:10, above). In other words, whereas ecclesiology dominates the composition of Ephesians, the focus of Colossians is—like Galatians—strictly christocentric.

Indeed, the ecclesiological focus of the author of Ephesians leads him to conjoin Christ and the church—a symbiosis that resembles the joining of husband and wife to "become one flesh" (5:31). Nevertheless the mystical union of Christ and the church does not fuse Christ and the church completely. The author never forgets that "the husband is the head of the wife just as Christ is the head of the church" (5:23, see also 1:22; 4:15; and Col 1:18; 2:19).

However, notwithstanding these wisdom reflections, we must notice that the speculative ideas of the letter have a pragmatic purpose, and in this respect the letter closely resembles Colossians. The author's ecclesiological and cosmic reflections are subordinate to the practical moral purpose of the upbuilding of the church, which pervades not only his ethical paraenesis (4:1–6:9), but also the letter as a whole (1:4, 12, 19; 2:1, 8-10; 3:17-19). Hence the author significantly elaborates the household codes that he derives from Colossians (5:2–6:9; see Col 3:18–4:1), and "Christianizes" them much more extensively than Colossians. His admonitions address not only wives and husbands (see Col 3:18-19) but also the "masters" of slaves (see Col 4:1; 5:22-33; 6:9). Moreover, the dualistic-apocalyptic texture of the final section of the letter (6:10-18) indicates how practical the focus of the author's ecclesiology is when he urges Christians to oppose in their daily life the hostile spiritual powers that rule the present world.

## THE PORTRAIT OF PAUL IN EPHESIANS

The portraits of Paul in Ephesians and Colossians coincide with their divergent theological perspectives.

To be sure, both letters share many features in their descriptions of Paul. Both portray Paul as the *solus apostolus*, both sketch him as the unique apostle to the Gentiles; and both picture him as the martyr who not only suffers (Eph 3:13; Col 1:24), but also is imprisoned for the sake of the gospel (Eph 3:1; 4:1; 6:20; Col 4:3, 10, 18). The dramatic words at the end of Ephesians and Colossians underscore this: "[the gospel] for which I am an ambassador in chains" (Eph 6:20); "Remember my chains" (Col 4:18).

However, whereas Colossians focuses on the Paul of wisdom who proclaims a cosmic Christ, Ephesians emphasizes the ecclesial Paul who is both a catholic liturgist and an ethical teacher. Moreover, Ephesians celebrates Paul the mystagogue, whose insight into the mystery of God's revelation surpasses that of all other apostles and prophets (3:4). His unique appointment to disclose this mystery has as its purpose to unite Gentiles and Jews into one body, the body of Christ (3:1-8; see also 2:1-22).

Ephesians portrays all this in a liturgical style and with a luxuriant overflow of language.[36] Moreover, the letter's incorporation of a multitude of early Christian liturgical and baptismal

traditions reflects a stage of Christian tradition that belongs to
a period much later than that of the historical Paul. In Ephesians,
then, the center stage is occupied by Paul, the ecclesial liturgist,
who sings the praises of the cosmic church.

When we realize that the Paul of Ephesians ascribes to
the church a universal-cosmic significance (1:20-23; 2:7; 3:10;
17-18; 4:10) and refuses to define the church as an apocalyptic
sect whose survival depends on its withdrawal from the world,
we cannot help but be surprised at the bold conception of the
author. We must remember that around the turn of the first
century A.D. the Christians of Asia Minor constituted only an
insignificant minority in an overwhelmingly pagan and hostile
world (5:16; 6:10-20).

Indeed, Paul's portrait in Ephesians conforms to its vision
of the church as the *una sancta catholica et apostolica ecclesia*.[37]
Paul is portrayed here as remembered by his pupils after his
death; a figure whose authority and stature have increased enor-
mously over time. He is now nostalgically transmitted to the
churches of Asia Minor as the apostle of sacred memory whose
struggles with Judaism and Judaizers have been forgotten and
whose apocalyptic yearnings have been displaced by an ecclesiology of triumphant eschatological fulfillment.

## *Paul's Legacy in 2 Thessalonians*

The theology of 2 Thessalonians is in many ways very
similar to that of 1 Thessalonians. One-third of 2 Thessalonians
borrows phrases and sentences from 1 Thessalonians, and their
similarity of structure is as striking as that of their themes.

### THE THEOLOGY OF 2 THESSALONIANS

The opening, body, and closing of both letters are almost
identical. The presence of a second thanksgiving (2 Thess 2:13;
1 Thess 2:13), which does not occur in any other letter of Paul,

is especially noteworthy. In fact, "2 Thessalonians contains no theme not found in 1 Thessalonians and both texts have the same central theme, namely eschatology."[38]

Indeed, the difficulty of comparing 2 Thessalonians with the historical Paul of 1 Thessalonians, and of getting hold of the specific theology of its author lies in his attempt to reduplicate Paul by copying as much as possible Paul's letter to the Thessalonians. However, although most English-language commentaries ascribe the letter to the historical Paul, many of its features demonstrate its post-Pauline character. In the first place, the eschatology of the author is quite different from that of Paul in 1 Thessalonians. Whereas Paul is engaged in stimulating the expectation of the parousia (1 Thess 4:13-18) and emphasizes the sudden and unexpected arrival of the day of the Lord (1 Thess 5:1-11), our author, in contrast, strenuously attempts to defuse apocalyptic excitement and announces that an apocalyptic timetable must run its course before the day of the Lord can occur (2:1-12).

Secondly, the warm and personal temper of 1 Thessalonians, which shows the intensely dialogical character of Paul's relation to his Thessalonian converts, shifts in 2 Thessalonians to an impersonal and didactic tone. Instead of Paul's personal "we give thanks" (*eucharistoumen*, 1 Thess 1:2; 2:13) and his pastoral "we exhort you" (*parakalein*, 1 Thess 2:11; 3:2, 7; 4:1, 10, 18; 5:11, 14), this author uses the formal and awkward phrase "we must always give thanks" (*opheilomen*, 1:3; 2:13) and the authoritative verb "we command" (*parangellein*, 3:4, 6, 10, 12), whereas he uses *parakalein* only twice (2 Thess 2:17 and 3:12 [but in 3:12 in conjunction with *parangellein*]). Thirdly, 2 Thessalonians frequently uses "Lord" (*kurios*) as a christological title. "The title occurs twenty-two times in the epistle, nine times associated with 'Jesus Christ' (1:1, 2, 12; 2:1, 14, 16; 3:6, 12, 16), four times with 'Jesus' (1:7, 8, 12; 2:8), eight times by itself (1:9; 2:2, 13; 3:1, 3, 4, 5, 16), and once in the expression 'the Lord of peace' (3:16).[39] This recurrent use of *kurios*, in conjunction with the author's stress on vengeance at the eschatological hour and his portrayal of Christ as the agent of the last judgment, not only eclipses Paul's theocentric perspective but also shows that "the christological emphasis of 2 Thessalonians falls on the future and . . . that Jesus' significance for the community also really lies in the future."[40]

Moreover, 2 Thessalonians demonstrates for the first time in Christian literature the existence of forged Pauline letters. Therefore the author warns repeatedly against such forgeries: "We beg you, brothers and sisters, not to be quickly shaken in mind or alarmed either by spirit or by word or by letter, as though from us (*di' epistolēs hōs di' hēmōn*), to the effect that the day of the Lord is already here" (2:1-2). This warning also guarantees the authenticity and authority of his own letter: "I, Paul, write this greeting with my own hand. This is the mark in every letter of mine; it is the way I write" (3:17).

In this context the author emphasizes the exceptional authority of "the traditions (*paradōseis*) that you were taught by us, either by word of mouth or by our letter" (2:15), and insists that the church must live in accord with "the tradition (*paradōsis*) that you received from us" (3:6). The paraenetic section of the letter (3:6-15) clearly shows why the author insists on the importance of "the tradition": it deals with the threat of disorder in the church (vv. 6-13) and with the need for church discipline (vv. 14-15). The verb "to command" (*parangellein*, 3:6, 10, 12), which dominates this section, reflects the author's concern that the church render "Paul" unquestioned obedience.

We can say, then, that the theology of 2 Thessalonians is marked by a slavish imitation of Paul's letter to the Thessalonians. Although the author follows Paul's hermeneutical method in relating the gospel's coherence to its contingency, his imitation of Paul is essentially anachronistic because he transposes Paul's gospel in 1 Thessalonians in an almost literal way to his own situation, which is quite different. And when he addresses his own situation in the apocalyptic program of 2:1-12 and in his warning against the asocial behavior of some Christians (*ataktoi*, 3:6-7, 11), he not only misrepresents the eschatological teaching of Paul in 1 Thessalonians, but also changes Paul's pastoral voice into that of an authoritarian.

## THE PORTRAIT OF PAUL IN 2 THESSALONIANS

Paul's portrait in 2 Thessalonians is the direct result of the imitative theology of the letter. Although in its characterization of Paul as the exclusive and authoritative apostle the portrait proves to be similar to that of the *P.E.*, Colossians, and Ephesians, the author of 2 Thessalonians imitates the Paul of 1 Thessalonians so closely that neither the distinctive marks of the Paul of the *P.E.* nor the creative reformulation of Paul in Colossians and Ephesians appear.

Nevertheless, the Paul of 2 Thessalonians possesses his own distinctive features. The author presents him as the apostle of absolute authority (although he employs neither the title "apostle" nor the first-person singular [except in 3:17]). He is an authoritative writer of letters, and both his written and spoken word demand obedience (2:15; 3:14, 17). "The pseudepigrapher's Paul is clearly an epistolographer, a man renowned as a writer of letters."[41] Moreover, Paul's authority manifests itself not only in his teaching and letter writing (see the emphasis on tradition, 2:15; 3:6, and on the verb "to command," 3:6, 10, 12), but also in his exemplary life-style.

Indeed, many features of the Paul of the other pseudepigraphical letters also surface in 2 Thessalonians. First of all, Paul's missionary toil and labor serve as an example to be imitated (*mimeisthai*, 3:7, 9; *typos*, 3:9).[42] Moreover, in these letters we receive a picture of Paul as the remembered apostle who is the exclusive source of Christian tradition and whose authority is evident both in his teaching and in his life-style.[43]

Besides these common features, 2 Thessalonians brings in one of its own: Paul, the theologian of the apocalyptic future. As Collins aptly remarks, "The Paul about whom our author writes is . . . not only a figure from the past. He is also an eschatological figure . . . within the perspective of a consequent or futuristic eschatology. . . . Addressing himself to the Thessalonians' hope for delivery from their afflictions, the author describes their salvation by means of the image of resting with Paul and his companions (*anesin meth' hēmōn*, 1:7). His portrait of Paul is a sketch of Saint Paul."[44]

# 4

## THE HISTORICAL PAUL AND HIS NEW TESTAMENT INTERPRETERS: A TRADITION-HISTORICAL APPROACH

### *Problems and Challenges*

It has been argued in this volume that the transmission of tradition faces the difficult but necessary task of determining whether "old" vocabularies and concepts can function within new time frames and different sociocultural contexts. In that context it was suggested that the category of adaptation can serve as a mediating agent in guiding the transposition of the *traditum* to new times and situations. Furthermore, it was pointed out that the criterion of appropriate faithfulness to the claim of the original *traditum* must determine whether adaptations are legitimate or illegitimate. As I mentioned earlier, the method of adaptation always faces the danger of transgressing its proper boundaries, which can lead to illegitimate adaptations whether in the form of anachronisms or acculturations (see pp. 30–31, above).

Before the criterion of appropriate faithfulness can be applied fruitfully to the post-Pauline writings, however, we must address the multiple ways in which this literature interprets Paul's legacy (see pp. 80–92, below). This multiplicity of Pauline portraits that emerges from the post-Pauline literature should not surprise us because each interpreter of Paul endeavors, in his own way, to translate the original tradition for the needs of his particular constituency.

In reflecting on the process of adaptation, some general observations about the reading of texts are in order. Readers of important and normative texts are not wont to engage in a scholarly reconstruction of "what it meant." Rather they are attentive to "what it means," i.e., to the meaning the text holds for their particular situation and needs.

In other words, "what it means" is the product of a dialogical encounter between reader and text. This encounter includes necessarily the insertion of the reader's own frame of reference (sociological, cultural, temporal) into her or his understanding of the text. Therefore, when we read a text, we acknowledge that it has a multivalent and polymorphous character and contains different levels of meaning. This is true whether it is interpreted by the same reader on different occasions or by many readers in different cultures and at different times.

In fact, the process of appropriating a text goes through several stages. Readers receive a text first of all by absorbing it within their own world or framework. Only after this absorption has been pondered and digested are readers able to verbalize the meaning of the text anew. And this re-production or re-actualization (*Vergegenwärtigung*) of the text must necessarily be expressed in the symbolic world that forms the reader's house of meaning.

When we apply these observations to post-Pauline writings, we must remember what was noted earlier (see pp. 35–36, above) about the insufficiency of employing the comparative method alone. Although this method has brought to light the considerable differences not only between Paul and his later New Testament interpreters but also among these interpreters themselves, it is inherently unable to be sensitive to the problems that the historicity of the tradition posed for these interpreters (see p. 79, below).

## The Adaptation of Paul's Tradition

We must be aware from the outset that the transmission of tradition can never achieve a pure recovery of the original *traditum* but must necessarily recast it. In other words, every adaptation can only be an approximation. Indeed, the quality of the recall and reactualization of the tradition must take into account fully the challenges that new times and situations demand. In other words, the interaction between the *traditum* and the *traditio* is a subtle one. It requires from the interpreter a finely honed perception to discern the adaptive ability of these post-Pauline authors in their endeavor to integrate the tradition with the needs and circumstances of their time. Although we must necessarily monitor how these adaptations appropriate the claims of the original tradition, this scrutiny is to be handled prudently; indeed, the constraints that the traditioning process exerted on these authors deserve to be explored case by case.

Therefore it is an error to absolutize the collective distance between these authors and the historical Paul, especially because their individual adaptive efforts vary greatly with respect to their creativity and relative distance from or proximity to Paul.

Many scholars succumb to such an absolutizing by adhering consciously or unconsciously to a theory of "the fall from the true Paul." In this manner recent proponents of the theory of "Early Catholicism" in the New Testament have viewed post-Pauline writings as a deplorable development that distorts true Paulinism. For instance, Käsemann's[1] adoption of a Pauline "canon within the canon" makes him insensitive to the necessities and challenges of the transmission of tradition and thus leads him to absolutize the distinction between the historical Paul and his post-Pauline interpreters.

However, once we realize that the distinction between
Paul and his New Testament interpreters must be drawn in a
flexible and sensitive manner, it will be possible to give a more
appreciative and historically sensible account of their adaptive
procedures.[2]

The post-Pauline writings exhibit a variety of adaptations
of Paul's legacy because each writing has a different perspective
on Paul's legacy. At least three factors determine their method
of adaptation: (1) the challenges of their particular circumstances; (2) their perception of what constitutes faithfulness to
the Pauline tradition; and (3) their imaginative or inept efforts
to reenact Pauline tradition for their own time.

In contrast to the sequence adopted in chapter 3, the
pseudepigraphal Pauline writings are now classified in terms of
their increasingly adaptive creativity:[3]

> 2 Thessalonians: adaptation as imitation of Paul
> The *P.E.*: adaptation as safeguarding a holy tradition
> Colossians and Ephesians: adaptation as creative refor-
> mulation of the Pauline tradition
> Acts: adaptation as a harmonizing rewrite of the Pauline
> tradition.

## 2 THESSALONIANS

The letter 2 Thessalonians illustrates a method of adaptation that seeks to duplicate Paul as much as possible. However, unlike the authors of the other pseudepigraphal letters,
this author refers to only one letter of Paul, 1 Thessalonians. In
fact, since one-third of the letter borrows phrases and sentences
from 1 Thessalonians, it is not surprising that many scholars
defend its Pauline authenticity.

The letter 2 Thessalonians demonstrates that the desire
to be faithful to Paul can actually turn into faithlessness when
it simply regurgitates Paul for a new set of circumstances. In
fact, 2 Thessalonians can hardly be called a dialogical letter

because it substitutes a didactic impersonal essay for Paul's intensely personal dialogue in 1 Thessalonians. As Gerhard Dautzenberg observes: "The orientation toward the authority and tradition of Paul is the basic point of view of the whole letter. It forms the redactional 'framework,' which permeates all the other components of the letter and which determines its total composition."[4]

However, as we saw earlier (see p. 73, above) the author provides his own teaching in 2:1-12, a section that gives us direct access to the situation and problems of his church. He is afraid that his people may be "shaken" and alarmed by utterances of the Spirit or by a letter supposedly coming from Paul, to the effect that "the day of the Lord is already here" (v. 2). The apocalyptic excitement of the church may well have been caused by intense apocalyptic expectations in the churches around the Mediterranean, evoked by the Jewish war against Rome (66–70 A.D.), the subsequent fall of Jerusalem, and the destruction of the temple in 70 A.D.

The author responds to this eschatological excitement with an apocalyptic timetable (2:1-12) and with a series of ethical admonitions (2:15–3:16). He has clearly a twofold objective in mind: (1) defusing the apocalyptic excitement of the church, and (2) reestablishing order in the church, which has been disturbed by church members who have abandoned their jobs and now sponge off of other Christians in anticipation of the apocalyptic hour (3:6-12).

The author issues these objectives in the name of Paul to give them special authoritative status. Indeed, Paul is not only portrayed as "a model to be imitated" (3:9; cf. 3:7), but also as the authoritative teacher whose teachings are normative and binding (see the emphasis on *paradosis* [2:15; also 3:6]).

It is indeed surprising that in the short period between 1 Thessalonians and 2 Thessalonians the Pauline tradition underwent such a decisive change. Although the author attempts to be faithful to the historical Paul in recalling the life-style and work of Paul and especially by incorporating many features of the Paul of 1 Thessalonians, he is forced to radically revise Paul's eschatology for the sake of the well-being of his church. We must remember that Paul's eschatological teaching in 1 Thessalonians meant to stimulate the expectation of the parousia and that he exhorted his people to "not fall asleep as others do, but let us keep awake and be sober" (5:6).

The author of 2 Thessalonians, to the contrary, attempts to defuse rather than stimulate the expectation of the parousia on account of the disorder that apocalyptic excitement causes in his church.

Indeed, whereas the readers of 1 Thess 4:13-18 are ignorant about important eschatological questions, those addressed in 2 Thessalonians 2–5 are well-versed in apocalyptic matters, for instance, in apocalyptic figures such as the antichrist and "the Restrainer."

We also must notice that 2 Thessalonians raises for the first time in Christianity the issue of Pauline letters. He not only refers several times to Paul's letter writing (2:2, 15; 3:14, 17), but also points to it in his greeting, which he writes "with my own hand. This is the mark in every letter of mine" (3:17; see Col 4:18; and in Paul's letters: 1 Cor 16:21; Gal 6:11; Philemon 19). His warning against falsified letters attributed to "Paul" demonstrates the great authority of Paul in some sections of the early church (2:15; 3:14) and may also indicate that already at this time forged letters of Paul were circulating.

How then shall we evaluate this author's adaptation of Paul? At this point it is important to remember that what Conzelmann observed about the *P.E.* applies not only to 2 Thessalonians but to all the post-Pauline writings; it merits repeating here: "[F]or an historical understanding it is not enough simply to confront the ethical ideal of the *P.E.* with the ethics of Jesus or Paul"; rather "it is necessary to consider the changed situation of the church and to interpret the *P.E.* together with contemporary writings (Luke and the Apostolic Fathers) in the context of a changing conceptual structure," because "change had to follow the reorientation toward a longer duration of life in the world."[5] Since the religious worldview and sociocultural situation of these writings are in many respects very different from those of Paul's own time, these authors seek to adopt innovative strategies that will make the historical Paul of the past a living word to the new situations and problems of their time. Indeed, they intend to be faithful to Paul's gospel in their own way because they are not interested at all in an academic reconstruction of the original Paul (see p. 43, above).

Therefore, although the author of 2 Thessalonians is much more rigid and wooden in his adaptation of Paul than the other pseudepigraphical Pauline authors, we must evaluate his efforts in terms of the constraints that the situation demanded. For instance, his pastoral concern is evident in the way he alters the emphases of 1 Thessalonians in his letter. He wants to convey Paul's fundamental authority to the contingent situation of his own church and thus calls upon Paul's life and authoritative teaching in order to consolidate his church. Thus he not only admonishes his church so that it can face its present situation of suffering in the world (1:4), but also commands it to banish "wicked and evil people" out of its midst (3:2; see 2:10). The author thus adapts Pauline tradition in such a way that he exhorts his people to cease their utopian speculation and to abandon their refusal to work, but rather to adopt a "quiet" disposition (3:12), inspired by "the steadfastness of Christ" (3:5).

## THE PASTORAL EPISTLES

When the reader recalls the unflattering comparison drawn between the historical Paul and the Paul of the *P.E.* (see pp. 38–43, above), there seems little room left for an appreciative appraisal of the adaptation of Paul's legacy by the Pastor. In comparing the Pastor's portrait of Paul with Paul's self-portrait, the result turned out to be quite negative. Indeed, the author's centripetal disposition, his preoccupation with church order and with orthodoxy, his delimitation of the gifts of the Spirit, and above all the priority of ecclesiology over eschatology—all these features seemed to dominate the Pastor's portrait of Paul. Thus, there seems to be ample reason to classify the

*P.E.* with its domesticated Paul as a distorted adaptation of Paul's legacy.

However, when we look at the Pastor's adaptation from a different perspective, his transmission of Pauline tradition deserves a more positive and sympathetic evaluation. In fact, from this perspective his adaptation of Paul must be judged to be quite successful, especially when we remember that many New Testament scholars attribute these letters—with or without appeal to a secretary-hypothesis—to the historical Paul.

We must not forget that the *P.E.* stem from a period in which history is experienced as an enduring reality and thus is perceived quite differently from Paul's conviction that "the appointed time has grown short" (1 Cor 7:29). The new experience of the prolongation of time is made more acute by the presence of two dangers that crucially affect the author's main concern. As we have seen (see pp. 44–45, above), dangers from without and from within threaten the order and stability of the church and jeopardize not only its survival and growth within the sociopolitical order of the Roman Empire, but also its inner cohesion and orthodoxy due to the inroads of heretics.

However, since the author—like most of the other early interpreters of Paul—intentionally refuses to delineate in a precise manner the contingent circumstances that engage his church, it is impossible to gain a clear picture of the situation to which he attempts to adapt the legacy of Paul. Indeed, as Hasler remarked (see p. 47, above), the *P.E.* combat the heretics rather than the heresy.

Notwithstanding the difficulty that this poses to the interpreters of the *P.E.*, the manner of the Pastor's adaptation of Paul's legacy gives us a clear picture of the basic themes and scope of his theological endeavor.

The situation in which the church finds itself calls for a tightening of the ranks. The gnostic speculation of the heretics (1 Tim 6:20) seems to be an attractive option for many church members (2 Tim 4:3) and appeals especially to women (1 Tim 5:11-15; 2 Tim 3:6-7). It seems that gnostic conventicles advocated egalitarian practices and permitted females an equal rank with males in the church (1 Tim 2:9-15).[6] Since the church is a fledgling and unstable community that houses "vessels" of all sorts (2 Tim 2:20), the author finds himself compelled to inculcate a strict order and to portray "Paul" as an uncompromising figure who not only teaches a rigid orthodoxy ("the sound doctrine" [1 Tim 1:10; 2 Tim 4:3; Titus 1:9; 2:1]), but also establishes a hierarchy of ministerial orders, proper ordination procedures, and rules for the succession of clergy. Indeed, a properly installed clergy must make sure that the Pauline tradition, which the author complements with a strict set of ethical rules and housecode-like ordinances (1 Tim 5:1-22), is transmitted to a reliable chain of successors (2 Tim 2:2; 1 Tim 5:17, 22). And so the author summarizes his conception of Paul's theology by using terms such as "deposit" (*parathēkē*, 1 Tim 6:20; 2 Tim 1:14) and "sound doctrine" (*hygiainousa didaskalia*, 1 Tim 1:10; 2 Tim 4:3). Brox explicates *parathēkē* as follows: "The term means in a literal sense that which is deposited or entrusted, that which one must conserve and hand back at the appropriate time. *Parathēkē* thus belongs to the specific language of tradition."[7]

Paul's adaptation, then, takes place against the background of the special conditions of the post-Pauline period in and for which the Pastor writes. As we have seen, he shares with all his contemporary Pauline interpreters a portrait of Paul, which nostalgic memory sketches in proportions larger than life: Paul, the hero and martyr, who single-handedly founded the churches of the Gentiles (see pp. 68, 72, above).

Moreover, the threat of the church's disintegration at the hand of speculative gnostic charismatics (2 Tim 2:17-18) coupled with the danger of a possibly intolerant outside world force the author to adapt Paul in the way he does. He has no use for Paul's passionate manner of doing theology or for Paul's lively dialogical engagement with his opponents. Rather he chooses to stress in a skewed manner those elements in Paul's letters that picture the apostle as an uncompromising, orthodox figure who does not tolerate being contradicted and who is constantly preoccupied with the orthodox unity of the church (see, for instance, Gal 1:1-10; 5:1-10; 1 Cor 4:18-21; 2 Cor 13:1-10). In short, the *P.E.* respond to the contingency of their situation with a coherent conception of the gospel which, however, only awkwardly intersects with the situation at hand. Therefore they portray Paul as a figure of unwavering orthodoxy whose pragmatic ordinances to his pupils and coworkers must guarantee the stability of the church. When we realize the troublesome circumstances of his time, we can understand that the Pastor's partisan and one-sided portrait of Paul is nevertheless a relevant rendering which, moreover, proved to be quite influential in subsequent church history.

Two observations by Brox help us to appreciate more adequately the Pastor's adaption of Paul: "The Pastoral Epistles can only be understood and correctly appraised within their historical-theological context if one pays attention to the enormous structural change (*Strukturwandel*) which the church experienced, with which it had to come to terms and which through its effort it had to transmit again to new generations. A new orientation of the 'old' became a necessity. It was here attempted and solved by allowing 'Paul' to speak in 'letters' to the contemporary church."[8] And again:

> And indeed when one allowed "Paul" to speak, it was done without simply repeating him. Rather one permitted him to speak in a way which was appropriate to the changed situation. It should be noted that this interpretation of Paul was not a conscious effort. However, precisely this interpretation of Paul understood Paul and his theology essentially better than a mere historicizing treatment of the apostle, which is sometimes the reason for the disparaging manner in which the Pastoral Epistles and their theology are treated by exegetes.[9]

## COLOSSIANS AND EPHESIANS

We have seen that 2 Thessalonians attempts to imitate Paul in a flat and unimaginative way and that the *P.E.* concentrate on portraying Paul as the guardian of the orthodox tradition. However, when we turn to Colossians and Ephesians, we notice a much more creative adaptation of Paul's legacy. Notwithstanding important theological differences between Colossians and Ephesians, they not only imitate closely the structure of Paul's letters and theology (see p. 69, above), but also compose a similar portrait of Paul. In fact, their imitation of Paul is so successful that many New Testament scholars have not hesitated to attribute both letters to the historical Paul.

Both letters emulate Paul in relating the indicative of the gospel to its imperative, i.e., in grounding the demand of the moral life in God's redemptive initiative in Christ. For instance, we read in Ephesians: "Husbands, love your wives as Christ loved the church and gave himself up for her" (5:25); and "Live in love, as Christ loved us and gave himself up for us" (5:2); or "For once you were darkness, but now in the Lord you are light. Live as children of light" (5:8). The same motif is sounded in Colossians: "Bear with one another and, if anyone has a complaint against another, forgive each other; just as the Lord has forgiven you, so you also must forgive" (3:13); and "So if you have been raised with Christ, seek the things that are above, where Christ is, seated at the right hand of God. Set your minds on things that are above, not on things that are on earth, for you have died, and your life is hidden with Christ in God" (3:1-3; see also 4:1: "Masters (*kyrioi*), treat your slaves justly and fairly, for you know that you also have a Master (*kyrion*) in heaven").

Moreover, the letters share many features in their portrayal of Paul. As noted above, the trend of the post-Pauline period sketches a Paul of sacred memory and paints him with extravagant colors. Thus, just like the *P.E.*, Ephesians and Colossians describe him as the sole apostle, as the one who has an incomparable "understanding of the mystery of Christ" (Eph 3:4), and who suffers martyrdom for the sake of the gospel (Col 1:24; 4:3, 10, 18; Eph 3:1; 4:1; 6:20). Indeed, their reformulation of Paul's gospel coupled with their heroic glorification of the apostle place these letters clearly in the period after Paul's death.

We must remember, however, that there are important differences between these letters. Whereas the author of Colossians is remarkably faithful to Paul in following his hermeneutical strategy of interweaving the gospel's coherent structure with the contingent situation, the author of Ephesians, to the contrary, dislodges the coherence of his gospel from any distinct contingent situation. In fact, New Testament scholarship has reached a virtual consensus in rejecting the letter's address to the Ephesians—not only because of the late attestation of the superscription ("To the Ephesians") and of the designation "in Ephesus" in the prescript, but also because of the impersonal character of the letter, its lack of any concrete details, and the absence of personal greetings to a community where Paul had been active for more than three years.[10] Indeed, the letter appears to be an encyclical treatise in the form of a letter addressed to a variety of churches in Asia Minor.

Thus, although Ephesians claims to be a letter from Paul, it lacks the occasional and particular specificity that characterizes Paul's letters and instead presents itself as a compendium of Paul's thought. Because of this feature, it resembles more closely the catholic letters of the New Testament than the letters of Paul. Furthermore, apart from the different manner in which Colossians and Ephesians relate the coherence of the gospel to its contingency, each letter has as well a distinct theological emphasis. We saw that Colossians is dominated by a christocentric theme and uses cosmic wisdom-language to combat the claim of speculative gnostic opponents, whereas Ephesians focuses on the theocentric aspect of Paul's theology and not only extols "the immeasurable greatness of his [God's] power for us who believe, according to the working of his great power. God put this power to work in Christ" (1:19-20a) but also celebrates the sovereign majesty of "the God and Father of our Lord Jesus Christ, who has blessed us in Christ with every spiritual blessing in the heavenly places" (1:3). And this praise of God climaxes in the glorification of his cosmic purpose "to gather up all things in him (Christ), things in heaven and things on earth" (1:10).

How then shall we appraise the adaptation of Paul's legacy in Colossians and Ephesians? First of all, we have already pointed to the remarkable correspondence between Colossians and Galatians on the one hand, and between Ephesians and Romans on the other hand (see p. 69, above). Colossians and Galatians alike concentrate on an exclusively christocentric focus, which— notwithstanding the disparity of their contingent situations— effectively counters syncretistic opposition.

Again at first glance both Ephesians and Romans appear to be compendia of Paul's thought rather than occasional letters. Moreover, both letters share a distinct theocentric focus, which aims at tracing the steps of God's universal salvation history. In fact, Melanchthon's sixteenth-century designation of Romans as a "compendium of Christian doctrine" has continued to influence greatly the interpretation of the letter even to this day. Indeed, as we noted already, Romans has in recent times been characterized as "a letter essay" (K. P. Donfried[11]) or as "the most mature statement of Paul's theology" (L. E. Keck[12]). In a similar way, we saw that scholars such as F. F. Bruce define Ephesians as "the quintessence of Paul's thought."[13] Indeed, both Ephesians and Romans exhibit a coherent-systematic structure, although recent scholarship increasingly recognizes that it is a mistake to characterize Romans as a non-occasional letter.[14] However, notwithstanding the fact that not only Colossians and Galatians, but also Ephesians and Romans share similar structures and theological themes, Colossians and Ephesians constitute, each in its own way, a transposition of Paul's thought and thus cannot qualify as letters of Paul. This is evident in their catholicizing tendencies and especially in their ecclesiology.

Ecclesiology is so primary in these letters that eschatology is subsumed under it. Indeed, we can say that a catholic portrayal of Paul emerges wherever the doctrine of the church is made the focal point of Paul's thought.[15] In this case, the upbuilding of the church, its ontological preexistent status, and its catholic destiny lead to a description of the church as *Christus prolongatus* (the extension of Christ), and as the *Corpus Christi mysticum* (the mystical body of Christ) so that the church constitutes the fulfillment of God's promises to Israel and the final goal of God's salvation history.

To be sure, although the church is as well a central part of Paul's theology, its function is determined by its relation to Paul's eschatology and Christology. For instance, whenever eschatology and Christology are conflated, the concept of the church is inflated and its identification with the future eschatological kingdom of God becomes a real danger. And the result is not only that a mystical doctrine of the church catholic displaces the idea of the church as a proleptic reality, but also that a spiritualization of God's promises displaces God's eschatological purpose for God's created world.

This danger becomes acute in both Colossians and Ephesians because the church has the status of a preexistent and posthistorical reality (Eph 1:4). Thus its ontological standing makes it an imperishable body that already participates in the divine world. Whereas Paul grounds God's eternal purpose and plan in the movement of salvation history from Christ to God's apocalyptic triumph (Rom 8:29; 1 Cor 15:49), the author of Ephesians adopts a realized eschatology of ecclesial fulfillment by an opposite movement, i.e., from Christ to the protological predestination of the church, which entails its eschatological fulfillment in the present (Eph 1:1-6). Within this scheme there is no room for Israel's eschatological salvation as a distinct people (see Rom 11:25-26). Instead Israel is now absorbed in the one church of Jews and Gentiles and ceases to exist as a separate entity (Eph 2:11-21).

Although Colossians attempts to retain the future eschatological outlook of Paul (3:1-3; cf. 1:5, 23), the letter coalesces Christ and the church in the manner of Ephesians, which means that Christ and the church cease to be separate entities. When Ephesians defines Christ as "the head" of the church, which is his "body" (1:22), and the church as "the fullness of him who fills all in all" (1:23), the author suggests that—since there can be no head without a body—the body of the church is located in heaven along with its risen head, Christ. The heavenly location of the church is confirmed by the fact that both authors stress that Christians have not only died with Christ but also have been raised with Christ to be "seated . . . with him in the heavenly places" (Eph 2:6; Col 2:12-13; cf. Col 1:13).

Notwithstanding these innovative adaptations of Paul's gospel, which manifest themselves in the catholicizing and ecclesiological emphases of these letters, the creative and imaginative reformulation of Paul's gospel for the needs of the authors' own time is quite remarkable. Although Ephesians does not imitate Paul in correlating the coherence of the gospel to its contingency, both writings bring Paul's gospel to bear upon the Hellenistic worldview of their time. Once we understand that Paul's temporal-horizontal (Jewish) eschatology is no longer deemed relevant within the contours of a worldview cast in spatial-vertical categories, it becomes clear that the cosmic coordinates in which Ephesians and Colossians translate their Christology represent a novel and creative adaptation of Paul's gospel (but see pp. 109–113, below).

## THE BOOK OF ACTS

Since Paul's portrait within the overall framework of Acts was discussed extensively in chapter 3, the appraisal of Luke's adaptation of Paul will be limited to a few remarks.

Luke intends to integrate his portrait of Paul harmoniously into his theme of the unity of the early apostolic church. However, this integration actually amounts to an accommodation and domestication of Paul; in short, it produces a homogenized Paul. In this context we must remember that—as this volume's portrayal of Paul's early interpreters has made clear—Paul's adaptation can take both a conservative and a radical form.

Indeed, in contrast to the radical adaptations of Colossians and Ephesians, Acts along with the *P.E.* and 2 Thessalo-

nians represents a conservative type of adaptation. Paul is portrayed in Acts as an obedient member of the one harmonious
apostolic church so that his gospel has no specific identity of its
own. Moreover, in sharp contrast to the Pauline pseudepigraphers, Acts denies Paul the apostolic title and ignores his letters.
Although Acts resembles the *P.E.* in describing Paul not only as
"culture-friendly" and a militant opponent of heretics but also
as a hero and martyr who actively strives for the unity of the
church, it is curious that, notwithstanding the common interests
of Acts and the *P.E.* in the consolidation and unity of the church,
Acts decisively differs from the *P.E.* in paying scant attention to
the matter of ministerial offices and ecclesial organization. Indeed, the book refers only three times to "elders" (presbyters)
and "overseers" (*episkopoi*, 14:23; 20:17, 28).

However, this disinterest of Luke in church organization
is not as puzzling as his peculiar portrayal of Paul. Notwithstanding his glowing admiration for Paul's missionary accomplishments, his Paul does not qualify as an apostle, has no distinctive kerygma, adopts an all-too-Jewish stance, and is a happy
member of the Jerusalem church. The precise reason for this
type of adaptation of Paul is unclear. It may be argued that in
Luke's time gnostic groups claimed Paul as their hero and that
Luke wanted to secure Paul for the legitimate apostolic church
by portraying him as an opponent of Gnostics and as a faithful
member of the church.[16] But in that case Luke certainly would
have portrayed Paul as a prominent antiheretical militant, which
he does not do, except for Paul's farewell address in chapter 20.

Therefore, we can only consider Luke's adaptation of Paul
an acute deformation and distortion of the historical Paul. What
is most surprising in this context is the great popularity that
Luke's portrayal of Paul has enjoyed throughout church history
and even in the church today. Indeed, the great influence of
Luke's portrait of Paul carries an important lesson for us: whenever the church is incapable of properly adapting the historical
Paul, it seems to be quite content with a pseudo-image of Paul,
such as Acts sketches.

# Similarities of Adaptation

The appraisal in this volume of the adaptive strategies of Paul's early interpreters has disclosed their multiple efforts to translate the Pauline tradition for the circumstances and needs of their particular constituencies. However, amid this wide variety of frequently imaginative reactualizations of the tradition, we must not lose sight of the many correspondences in their portrayal of Paul. These common features in their adaptation of Paul demonstrate the similarity of the theological problems that they had to face. Indeed, the list of like affirmations in the pseudepigraphal Pauline letters is extensive.[17] All of them stress these points:

1. The unique character of Paul's apostolate and the unquestionable authority of his exclusive and "orthodox" gospel.

2. Paul's exclusive merit in founding the churches of the Gentiles.

3. A portrait of Paul as the suffering martyr, whose commitment to the gospel is sealed by his suffering and death.

4. A movement toward a special Pauline canon, limited to his letters. Although this process anticipates Marcion's canon in the second century A.D., it would certainly reject Marcion's dismissal of the Old Testament. Nevertheless the nearly complete neglect of the Old Testament by these authors is quite remarkable.

5. An increasing glorification of Paul, now painted as a heroic figure, demonstrating how nostalgic memory has affected his portrayal in the time after his death. Indeed, Acts, notwithstanding its exceptional status among the New Testament interpreters of Paul, shares in this glorification of Paul with a host of stories, celebrating his impressive rhetoric and miraculous deeds.

6. A description of Paul as *(a)* a "culture friendly" person and/or *(b)* as a political sympathizer with Rome. Colossians, Ephesians and the *P.E.* sketch him as "culture-friendly," since they incorporate Roman household codes and secular social norms in their letters, whereas Acts, and less so the *P.E.*, describe him as a person who seeks ways to establish an accommodation with the state.

7. A picture of Paul, the polemical antiheretical and orthodox apostle, who does not tolerate any deviation from his gospel.
8. A characterization of Paul as the champion of the unity and consolidation of the church.[18]

Martin Elze has correctly observed that the unity of the church was the focus of the church in the second century A.D. and that theological diversity served that purpose.[19] But already at the end of the first century A.D. the Pauline pseudepigraphers show that this motif actually overshadows all other theological issues. The unity motif is especially clearly expressed in Ephesians: "There is one body and one Spirit, . . . one Lord, one faith, one baptism, one God and Father of all" (4:4-6).

Since the issues and theological premises of Paul's time were no longer directly applicable or useful to the circumstances of the post-Pauline authors, they sketched Paul not only as a figure who advocates peaceful coexistence with the political and social order of Rome and who incorporates elements of Roman family life into the life of the church, but also as an apostle who champions the unity of the church by combatting and even excommunicating heretics (1 Tim 1:20; 2 Tim 4:14, 15; Titus 3:10, 11 [*hairetikos anthrōpos*]). Above all, the portrayal of Paul as the sole apostle to the Gentiles serves to emphasize that his exclusive gospel forms the basis of the unity of the church.

Above all, we must be aware that one central focus underlies all of the multiple adaptive strategies employed by the post-Pauline authors: the creation of a "catholic" Paul.

# The Necessity and Shortcomings of the Comparative Approach

I have argued that the comparative method performs a necessary task because, in safeguarding the claim of the original Pauline tradition, it must evaluate the adequacy of its adaptation by Paul's tradents (the transmitters of Pauline tradition) in the

New Testament. In tracing the comparisons between the *traditum*, i.e., the authentic gospel of Paul, and the *traditio*, i.e., the traditioning process, we have discovered that most of the post-Pauline authors fall short of translating Paul's gospel properly. In the first place, most post-Pauline writings misrepresent or disregard Paul's most distinctive theological contribution, i.e., the opportune interplay between the gospel's coherence and its situation-specific contingency. Even when they address contingent situations, they portray Paul either as an authoritative, dogmatic figure who refuses to enter into dialogue with his opponents (for example, the *P.E.*) and who imposes his unquestionable teaching on his church (for example, 2 Thessalonians, along with all the other Pauline pseudepigrapha), or as a figure who defuses the real point of view of his opponents (Colossians), or as a theologian who simply issues a general theological treatise (Ephesians). The portrait of Paul in Acts in particular shows the extent to which the author misunderstands both Paul's message and his method.

In the second place, the inevitable consequence of this misrepresentation of Paul's hermeneutical method is the suppression of the contingent features of Paul's theologizing. In this context we must note that the suppression of contingent situations is not an oversight, but rather an essential part of the attempt by Paul's tradents to universalize Paul's letters so that a catholic Paul can be transmitted to subsequent times.

However, notwithstanding the comparative method's necessary task of correcting basic misappropriations of the historical gospel of Paul, the method contains some severe shortcomings. Its historicizing procedure precludes consideration of the factors involved in the tradition-process, as well as of the necessities of adaptation. In overlooking the inevitability of linguistic change and social and historical development, it is susceptible to all the dangers of a docetic interpretation. Thus it tends to produce a myopic and one-sided view of the adaptive accomplishments of Paul's interpreters.

Indeed, the comparative method decontextualizes not only the original Pauline tradition, but also its necessary adaptation by Paul's tradents. Therefore the method is inherently unable to take into account the problems and challenges that the transmission of tradition must face, i.e., the problems that the historicity of tradition evokes and the challenges that call for an imaginative recasting of the tradition. For instance, when the comparative method compares persons and events from markedly different historical periods, it overlooks not only the necessary modifications of the tradition that later times demand, but also the often creative and imaginative ways in which later interpreters adapted Paul's gospel to make it living speech for the needs of their time once again.

Illustrations of the shortcomings of such an exclusive use of the comparative method can be found easily, for instance, in the comments of two patristic scholars. The first is Franz Overbeck's famous saying that "In the second century nobody understood Paul except Marcion, who misunderstood him."[20]

In a similar fashion, Eva Aleith comments on the adaptation of Paul in the patristic period:

> The institution of the ancient church does not want to be Petrine or Pauline, but apostolic. Because of this, it cannot use any extreme genius and outsider. The diligent way in which Paul as representative of the harmonious company of the apostolic college and as a faithful member of a uniform tradition is represented, is therefore not so strange, because the understanding of the particularity of Pauline theology is actually absent. We cannot discover any trace of the Pauline teaching of sin and redemption in the early Christian apologists. The doctrine of the seminal logos and the freedom of will favor a consistent moralism. None of the old theologians was able to penetrate into the essence of Paul's teaching of faith. The apologists learned nothing else from the post-apostolic writings, but that faith was a free assent to doctrine, and subsequent times would add little to this. Paul experienced as hardly any other writer the fate to be read diligently and with admiration, but to be rarely understood.[21]

It is clear from these comments that these authors have no sensitivity either to the difficulties that the transmission of tradition poses or to the challenges that new historical circumstances and altered worldviews impose on tradents.

Therefore a comparative method must be balanced and corrected by employing a traditio-historical method. The latter views Paul's adaptations by his later tradents as holistic texts in their own right, which ought not only be compared with the historical Paul, but deserve also to be evaluated in terms of the realistic demands and possibilities that their own historical location imposed on them.

# 5

## PAUL'S IMPACT ON THE POST-PAULINE PERIOD AND ON THE CHURCH TODAY

AT THE COMPLETION of this journey through the post-Pauline writings, the question arises whether the exploration of the multiple adaptations of Paul's legacy by his New Testament interpreters merely represents an academic exercise, possibly important for New Testament scholars in their attempt to reconstruct the history of the early church but of little relevance to the church today. In fact, this inquiry may be dismissed as superfluous not only by readers who cling to a long-standing tradition that the Pauline pseudepigrapha are actually authentic letters of Paul, but also by an opposite group of readers who considered these writings all along to be a deplorable fall from the true Paul.

## *The Esteem for Paul in the Church Today*

However, it is my contention that the reception of Paul by his New Testament interpreters has great importance for the church today. Since the church accords canonical status not only to Paul's authentic letters but also to the letters of his apostolic pupils in the New Testament, they constitute together an essential part of the written word of God in Scripture, which we confess to be the normative source of Christian life and doctrine (see, for instance, the 1967 Confession of the Presbyterian Church in the USA: "Scripture is the Word of God written"). In other words, these writings do not comprise an archaeological deposit but are confessed to convey the power of the gospel ever anew to different times and circumstances.

However, if Scripture in fact has this authority, a serious problem difficult to resolve confronts us. How, for example, do we draw the line between the abiding-normative elements of Paul's gospel and its contingent, time-bound elements? Indeed, when we endeavor to interpret Paul to our churches today we somehow realize that it is impossible to bestow authoritative status on all of his pronouncements. We realize that his statements about marriage, sex, homosexuality, women, slaves, and so on seem so culturally determined and dated that they can hardly qualify as an abiding word of God.

To be sure, the delineation between the abiding coherence of Paul's gospel and its contingent elements often involves us necessarily in subjective judgments because what is contingent for one interpreter is frequently an inherent part of the coherence of the gospel for another. However, we must realize that a catalytic hermeneutic of Paul's gospel can deal with these problems more successfully than a literalistic hermeneutic. For whereas a catalytic hermeneutic acknowledges the necessity of having to distinguish between the abiding or coherent elements of Paul's gospel and its time-conditioned interpretations, a literalistic hermeneutic does not draw such a distinction, but rather ascribes normative authority in a simplistic, anachronistic manner to all of Paul's statements.

Even apart from such specific hermeneutical concerns, today's preachers and teachers must deal with a much more burdensome problem. Indeed, a large-scale alienation from Paul's gospel coupled with a widespread dislike for the person of Paul seem to prevail in our churches. Karl Barth's talk of the "Strange New World within the Bible" seems to have become so true for many of us with respect to Paul that he actually no longer concerns us. I ascribe this estrangement from Paul not only to this dislike for his temperamental and high-strung personality, but especially to the difficulty we have in appropriating his gospel, i.e., in experiencing its relevance for our lives today. Indeed, it is simply quite difficult for people today to relate either to Paul's message or to his person. In fact, we all too often seem to exchange one annoyance for another: We attribute the unintelligibility of Paul's message to the unpleasant impression that his person evokes in us, or, conversely, we dislike Paul's personality so intensely that we refuse to pay attention to his message.

Whenever I meet in continuing education sessions with members of the clergy, I regularly inquire what sections of Scripture they single out in their preaching. And when they point without exception to the Gospels and to some of the Old Testament prophets, I ask them why they omit the letters of Paul. They usually respond by complaining about "the difficult Paul," especially about the trouble they have in conveying to their people the argumentative texture of his letters and the seeming irrelevance of many of Paul's concerns. To be sure, the preachers' preference for the Gospels and sections of the Old Testament is understandable because—as noted earlier (see p. 27, above)— narrative texts lend themselves more readily to intelligible interpretation and relevant transposition than epistolary texts, especially when epistolary texts are occasional-dialogical products rather than philosophical essays in letter form.

Moreover, many intelligent church members cherish a dislike for Paul because of his presumable arrogance, his doctrinal stance, or his "perversion" of the gospel of Jesus. The legacy of Ernst Renan and Friedrich Nietzsche, for whom Paul was an enemy of the gospel of Jesus and a "dysangelist," seems to be very much alive in the church today. It sometimes appears as if Paul's gospel is used in the church only on Reformation

Sunday (Rom 1:16-17), for weddings (1 Corinthians 13) and
for funerals (Rom 8:31-39)!

What is at stake here is essentially the question of how—
in Gotthold E. Lessing's words—we bridge the "ugly ditch"
between the past and the present. In other words, is it possible
for us to relate properly the *traditum*, the deposit of the tradition,
to the *traditio*, the process of tradition? The various ways in
which interpreters have endeavored to relate—in Krister Stendahl's formulation—"what a text meant" to "what it means"
shows how difficult it is to bridge this "ugly ditch."

In facing this urgent problem, we naturally look for biblical scholarship to come to the rescue. But New Testament
scholars rarely help in bridging the gap between past and present.
Convinced of their success in penetrating the mind and social
location of first-century authors with nearly perfect historical
results, New Testament scholars usually consider themselves
exclusively committed to "what it meant." In other words,
whether driven by a sense of scholarly integrity or by a com-
pulsion to impress members of the biblical guild, often they
seem interested only in addressing an increasingly smaller circle
of fellow specialists. It is easy to wonder how useful scholarly
New Testament commentaries are to the pastor. Pastors may be
interested in exploring, for instance, the precise meaning of the
"righteousness of God" in Romans. But what often happens is
that after reading page after page about the nature of the genitive
in that phrase, they experience more confusion after consulting
the commentary than when they started—especially when a dil-
igent commentator offers the reader a fruit salad of options on
each significant grammatical issue.

It is not intended here to disparage the necessary work
or the integrity of contemporary scholarship, but instead to view
the matter from the perspective of the conscientious pastor in
his or her task of adapting Scripture to the needs of a congre-
gation. In other words, when biblical scholarship shuns the task
of bridging the gap between past and present, it not only shuns
the total range of the hermeneutical task but also arrogates to

itself—strangely enough—an ahistorical stance because historians must realize that they themselves are involved in the historicity of life and language. Ebeling makes an important comment on this issue. In a dispute with Bultmann's view, which argues that historical-critical objectivity should be divorced from an existential encounter with the biblical text, Ebeling writes: "The split *between* the historical-critical method in contemplating the text from a distance *and* the existential hearing of the text as personal address cannot do justice either to the inner unity of the hermeneutical process or to its differentiation."[1]

But what about those biblical scholars who, dedicated to the task of adaptation, are attempting to bridge the gap between what it meant and what it means—i.e., the gap between the historical Paul and the present time—so as to counter the anti-Pauline sentiment in the church? At this point all that will be discussed is one type of contemporary adaptation, that which may be considered popular adaptations of Paul's gospel.

The attempt is made here to universalize Paul's contingent theological statements to make them existentially relevant. For instance, Robin Scroggs in his *Paul for a New Day* uses Norman O. Brown's interpretation of Freud[2] in his own existential exposition of Paul. Scroggs writes: "For both Brown and Paul, authentic life consists in a return to an original situation made possible by the risk of giving up striving for selfhood and by accepting selfhood, rather, as something already present."[3]

Another example of such a popular adaptation is presented by Lucas Grollenberg, O. P., in *Die moeilijke Paulus* ("That Difficult Paul"). Grollenberg thinks he can simplify Paul for today's readers by suggesting that an underlying essence undergirds Paul's difficult arguments, namely, Paul's mystical union with the divine.

However, we must realize that such attempts are bound to fail because they ignore the fact that Paul's gospel is determined by two factors: (1) the intricate interplay between coherence and contingency, and (2) its inherent historicity. Therefore, such modernizing updatings of Paul are engaged in misleading analogies and constitute misrepresentations of Paul's gospel. They demonstrate that the adaptation of Paul's gospel to new historical and sociocultural periods is fraught with formidable obstacles.

## Paul's Legacy in the New Testament Church

The adaptation of Paul's legacy for new historical situations is not a free choice but an unavoidable necessity. Brox expressed this necessary adaptation very clearly when he argued that, since the *P.E.* must be seen as a contemporary form of Pauline interpretation, they attempted to make "Paul" speak not simply by repeating him in a literal manner, but rather in a manner which was appropriate for the changed situation.[4]

### ADAPTATION: ITS NECESSITY AND PROBLEMS

When we realize that adaptation is preeminently occupied with the problem of the continuity of tradition amid the discontinuities of history, its necessity becomes evident. What other means does the church have to safeguard the continuation of its identity in relation to itself and to the world when it finds itself in a new location in history and must appropriate its foundational tradition for situations for which it was not intended?

Indeed, whenever adaptation succeeds in achieving a new *Sprachgestalt* (linguistic expression) of the *Sachverhalt* (material content) of the tradition, the difficult problem of re-presenting the tradition is overcome. Therefore, the necessity of adaptation is not only a burden but also contains a promise. Indeed, its ability to re-actualize the claim of the tradition for new times and circumstances gives the tradition new power of speech.

However, when we remember not only the inherent historicity of Paul's idiom and conceptuality but also the idiosyncratic and passionate manner in which he relates the coherence of the gospel to its various contingencies, the possibility of a successful adaptation of Paul's gospel seems to evaporate. In fact, the story of the authentic adaptation of Paul's gospel has been largely a story of failure in the history of the church.

And when we have to face it anew in the present time, we must realize that we cannot hope to resolve the problem without the help of Paul's early interpreters. Notwithstanding the great temporal distance separating us from them, they are our earliest predecessors in this venture. Indeed, the significant variations in their adaptation of Paul demonstrate not only the burden of tradition but also its challenges and promises. To be sure, this investigation has shown that their failures in authentically adapting Paul certainly outweigh their successes.

However, the important issue here is the fact that they understood the necessity of the task. Nearly all of them realized that Paul's gospel could not be reproduced literally but had to be reinterpreted for the crises and needs of their own day. And so they pose the urgent question to us: Does the church today equally understand the necessity and challenge of adapting Paul to its own situation in the world?

## PAUL AND HIS EARLY INTERPRETERS

We must now determine in what sense Paul's early interpreters can provide us with guidelines for his adaptation in the church today. In this discussion the order adopted in chapter 3 will be followed, except for the treatment of Acts (see p. 35, above).[5]

### The Pastoral Epistles

The *P.E.* endeavor to adapt Paul's gospel by transmitting it in a conservative and rigid manner. Before we dismiss their adaptation too quickly on this ground, we must remember that the Pastor offers the contemporary church an attractive solution to the problem of the transmission of Paul's gospel.

Since Paul's own hermeneutic is shaped by the intricate interaction of coherence and contingency, and since the substance of his gospel is directly related to the specific controversies

of his own time, the Pastor attempts to make Paul relevant to
his situation by universalizing and diffusing the basic character
of Paul's hermeneutical method. This type of adaptation appeals
to us because the divorce of the coherence of Paul's gospel from
its contingent address enables us to transmit a catholic-doctrinal
Paul, who is relevant "everywhere, always and to everyone" (see
the definition of what is catholic by Vincent of Lerinum in his
*Commonitorium* [434 A.D.]: *Quod ubique, quod semper, quod
ab omnibus creditum est* [What everywhere, always and by all
persons is believed]). Indeed, Paul's gospel constitutes authoritative and normative tradition not only for the Pastor, but also
for us.

   Although the Pastor differs from us in that he limits the
Christian tradition to Paul's gospel alone, both he and we attempt
to make that gospel a relevant word on target for new situations
and different worldviews. The claim that the Pastor truly imitates
Paul in interweaving coherence and contingency seems to have
some validity. He does not simply reproduce the bygone contingencies of Paul's time, but rather endeavors to apply Paul's theological convictions to the new circumstances of his church. But
this claim cannot be upheld. In proposing a timeless coherence
of the gospel, the Pastor bifurcates its coherent and contingent
components and thus perverts Paul's dialogical method. Indeed,
as seen earlier, the coherence of the gospel is quite artificially
related to its contingent situation in the *P.E.* Instead of engaging
his heretical opponents, the Pastor dismisses their claims out-
right, vilifies them, and does not permit discussions with them
(see 2 Tim 2:14-23; Titus 1:10-16).

   The *P.E.*, then, transform the historical Paul into a dogmatic Paul who imposes his teaching on his audience and displaces dialogical conversation with authoritative monologue.

   And so the *P.E.* illustrate vividly how difficult it is for
later interpreters to solve the problem of the particularity of
Paul's letters. In fact, the *P.E.* are not far removed from the
solution that the framers of the canon adopted. We noticed that
they likewise diffused the particularity of Paul's letters to transmit a catholic Paul. And yet, contrary to the Paul of the New

Testament canon, the *P.E.* honor Paul's exclusive status as apostle and teacher. It would have been unthinkable for the Pastor to imitate the framers of the canon by placing the Catholic Epistles before Paul to produce a harmonized Paul to facilitate a universal-catholic understanding of Paul.

It is important to realize that the adaptation and appropriation of Paul's gospel in the church today is much closer to the Pastor's portrait of Paul than to Paul's self-portrait in his letters. Indeed, the hermeneutical solution of the *P.E.* appeals to us because it is so much easier for us to appropriate the simple authoritative Paul of the *P.E.* than the difficult Paul of the letters.

We have truly become heirs to the tradition of a dogmatic Paul, which has dominated church history and continues to determine our adaptation of Paul. The Paul we transmit in our preaching and teaching is usually composed of a collection of his orthodox key terms, often presented in the form of proof texts, which, divorced from their historical context, must somehow be made to fit our own historical context.

And even when we try to unravel Paul's complicated and frequently abstruse arguments—for instance his allegory about Hagar and Sarah against the Judaizers in Galatia (Gal 4:21-31) or his attack against women with unveiled heads in the worship service (1 Cor 11:2-10)—we are genuinely puzzled how these arguments of Paul can be religiously relevant to today's church, which feels itself alienated from problems that do not touch its existence and seem confined to the first century A.D.

Paul's adaptation by the *P.E.*, then, tempts us to treat the historical Paul similarly. Once we become aware of the historicity of all theological statements and thus of the problems inherent in the transmission of tradition, the adaptive move of the Pastor seems to us not only a necessary move, but even a welcome move.

Indeed, he has bequeathed to us a Paul who is capable of universal application, and who, moreover, addresses a series of contingent problems, which are not only those of his time, but still concern us deeply. After all, the Pastor deals with concerns that we sorely miss in the letters of the historical Paul. He deals extensively with matters such as church administration, the appointment of clergy, its hierarchical status and its reliable succession. He also organizes proper liturgical orders and does not tolerate any subversion of the tradition or any deviant moral behavior. Indeed, these subjects have provided us and still furnish us with important guidelines with respect to church polity, especially when we remember not only the controversy between the Reformed churches and the Roman Catholic church about the status of bishops, elders, and deacons, and their succession, but also our concern about the ordination of women in the church. The trend started by the *P.E.* in not allowing women a full ministry in the church has had enormous influence on subsequent church history.

The church in the *P.E.* wants to be in the world, not of the world. But it lives in a world that, contrary to Paul's expectation, will be around for quite a while. Thus new relations between church and world must be established. The church must deal not only with matters of inner cohesion (polity) and organization in view of the danger of heresy, but also with proper relations to the state.

Again, the problem of the relation of the church to culture and the state is also of deep concern to us today. Since most of us consider Paul's expectation of the imminent end of history no longer a viable option, we—like the Pastor—are preoccupied with the relation of Christ and culture and with the manner in which this relation must be defined.

The *P.E.* handle these issues by employing a twofold strategy that advocates consolidation and accommodation. Consolidation must secure institutional order within the church (see above), while accommodation must safeguard its relations to the outside world. Indeed, the *P.E.* show increasing concern about public relations, sensitivity to outsiders, a good reputation (cf. "good works") and a rapprochement with local civic authorities and with the state (1 Tim 2:1-2). Within this context Paul is portrayed as an institutional organizer and implacable dogmatician who struggles for the pragmatic survival and growth of the church.

## Ephesians and Colossians

When we turn to Ephesians and Colossians, we notice that these letters not only breathe an atmosphere of ecumenicity, but also show considerable intellectual originality. Thus, in contrast to the *P.E.*, who present Paul as a rigid, pragmatic organizer and his theology as a collection of orthodox statements, both Ephesians and Colossians represent creative and authentic adaptations of Paul's legacy.

This is especially true for Ephesians. We have seen that many scholars sing its praises. Besides F. F. Bruce (see p. 69, above), other scholars join this chorus. For instance, Bruce M. Metzger writes: "In any case, whoever wrote the letter and wherever it was addressed, Ephesians is one of the most exalted of the writings of the New Testament. Its theme is God's eternal purpose in establishing and completing the universal church of Jesus Christ."[6] And Luke Johnson adds: "In Ephesians we find a masterly statement on the work of God in the world and church, expressed not by the passion of polemic or the logic of argumentation, but by prayerful mediation."[7]

Indeed, Ephesians—with its cosmic-universal ecclesiology, its celebration of "the immeasurable greatness" of God's power, and its theme of the reconciliation of Jew and Gentile (2:11-21)—has an extraordinary appeal to our ecumenical age. It offers us a creative reformulation of Paul's thought, which is all the more attractive because it manages to present "the quintessence of Paulinism" (F. F. Bruce) in a profound and cohesive way.

However, we must not forget that the very feature of Ephesians that appeals to us most disqualifies it in some ways as a faithful rendering of Paul's thought. The encyclical character of the letter demonstrates that the most crucial aspect of Paul's theologizing, i.e, the interplay between coherence and contingency, is here virtually ignored. Thus Ephesians sacrifices the particularity of Paul's theology for the sake of a catholic-universalism, which makes possible a smooth transmission of Paul's doctrinal gospel to every subsequent historical epoch.

Therefore, although our habit of viewing Ephesians as "the quintessence of Paul's thought" has great appeal, it betrays in three ways a basic ignorance of what is most Pauline in Paul's theology: (1) the coherence of the letter has no relation to any clear contingency, be it that of heretical dangers or political threats; (2) the letter shifts Paul's theological focus toward a different center; and (3) it also misinterprets some crucial elements of Paul's thought.

Although Ephesians intends to transmit Pauline tradition, it misunderstands Paul's concept of grace. Indeed, grace is not only combined with a realized eschatology, but also associated with "good works": "For by grace you *have been saved* (*sesōsmenoi*) through faith. . . . For we are what he has made, created in Christ Jesus for good works (*epi ergois agathois*)" (2:8, 10). This misunderstanding is all the more evident in light of Paul's use of the verb "to save" (*sōzō*), which almost always refers to the eschatological future, as well as in the non-Pauline phrase, "good works" (*erga agatha/kala*), a notion that appears frequently in the post-Pauline writings.

Moreover, as pointed out earlier (see p. 72, above), the author's focus on the universality of the apostolic-catholic church subordinates Paul's eschatology to his ecclesiology and displaces this eschatology with the concept of the "divine commonwealth" (C. H. Dodd). This subordination of eschatology to the church contradicts the priority of the eschatological triumph of God in Paul because Paul defines the church as the anticipation of God's triumph and not as its realization.

Nevertheless, we can rightfully claim that Ephesians offers a creative adaptation of Paul's legacy. In a time when Paul's imminent expectation of God's coming final glory was no longer the object of fervent hope, the author of Ephesians intends to be faithful to Paul's legacy by construing the coherence of Paul's gospel so that it might speak to the concerns of his day. In concert with the other pseudepigraphical Pauline authors, he not only insists on Paul's exclusive status among the apostles (2:20; 3:5) and on the sole authority of his gospel (3:2-6), but also surrounds

Paul with the halo of a supreme witness and martyr. As mentioned before, this glorification of the apostle can be expected from authors in the post-Pauline era who gratefully remember that Paul was responsible for founding their Gentile churches. And so this author transmits Paul's gospel by redesigning its central elements to serve his own purpose. However, as we have seen, his vision of the cosmic nature of the church with its emphasis on the steady growth of the church in the world are portrayed in a somewhat general and abstract manner, since the author deals with specifics only when he incorporates a list of household codes into his work (see, for instance, his very general remarks about various ministerial functions in 4:11-16).

And he conveys all this in a style that, although cumbersome with its long-flowing sentences and idiomatic plethora, conveys the meditative and prayerful mood of the author, who prefers a liturgical style over the often polemical and argumentative manner of Paul.

Ephesians, then, not only offers promising opportunities but also significant questions for Paul's adaptation by the church today. Although the author's adaptation signifies a creative reformulation of Paul's legacy, which no doubt is the reason for the letter's popularity in our churches, the letter nevertheless raises the question whether we can truly be satisfied with his reformulation of Paul's thought. Does not the supposed advantage of the letter—i.e., its straightforward, coherent structure and its easy access to Pauline doctrine—in fact represent a disadvantage? We have noted that the lack of a specific contingent target severely decontextualizes the letter and turns it into an abstract product.

Moreover, can we really surrender the eschatological vision of Paul and its ethic of solidarity with God's whole creation? Does not this surrender in Ephesians entail a concept of the church that celebrates its own salvation so much that it disregards the rest of the world?

Ephesians then presents the church today with a challenge and an obligation. It challenges us to imitate the creativity of the author in his adaptation of Paul and at the same time obliges us to not simply repeat his particular version of Paul.

As we have seen, Colossians was written before Ephesians, and in many ways determines the theology and composition of that letter. Indeed, Colossians shares many features with Ephesians. Apart from their mutual stress on Paul's exclusive status, they both adopt not only a vertical conception of eschatology and the notion of the church as a heavenly entity, but also the conviction that Christians have already been raised with Christ into heaven (Col 2:12; 3:1; Eph 2:4-6).

And yet we saw that, notwithstanding these agreements, Colossians develops its own theological focus: It emphasizes the exclusivity of a cosmic Christ in the letter's polemic against the claims of the supplementary Christology of the Colossian heretics.

We must be aware, however, that our contemporary adaptation of Colossians with its "Pauline" message is a difficult matter. In contrast to Ephesians and its lack of a specific contingency, Colossians closely imitates Paul's theological method. Therefore it presents to the contemporary church the same dilemma that the adaptation of the authentic Pauline letters poses. The close interplay between coherence and contingency in Colossians demands of the church today that it imitate the author of Colossians in confronting the speculative heresies of our time with a similar either-or stance.

Our usual way of solving the problem of the adaptation of Colossians is, however understandable, quite deficient. On the one hand, we decontextualize those parts of the letter that seem of universal importance, whereas on the other hand we historicize the passages we consider to be outdated. For instance, we emphasize the universal importance of the christological texts of Colossians, texts such as: "For in him [Christ] all the fullness of God was pleased to dwell" (1:19; see also 2:3, 15; 3:1-3). In a similar manner we cite with approval the general claims of the ethical portions of Colossians such as "Do not lie to one another seeing that you have stripped off the old self with its practices and have clothed yourselves with the new self" (3:9-10; see also 3:5-17). However, when we have to deal with the household codes of Colossians (Col 3:18–4:1; cf. Eph 5:22–6:9), we abruptly surrender this catholicizing-universal method of adaptation and withhold from these texts any normative status for the church today because of their dated character.

Because the problems that occasional letters such as Colossians and the letters of Paul present require an urgent solution, it will be argued in a subsequent section that the issue of their contingency is capable of a solution once we recognize that it is possible to transcend their specific time-conditioned character (see pp. 122–24, below).

## 2 Thessalonians

The author of 2 Thessalonians deserves to be called a copyist since he defines adaptation as a repristination and an almost literal imitation of Paul. The method the author uses to adapt Paul to his post-Pauline situation is quite curious. As we have seen, he repeats several times that he writes a Pauline letter (2:2, 15; 3:14, 17). Moreover, he informs his church that true Christian tradition is exclusively Pauline, so that it must be faithful to "the traditions that you were taught by us, either by word of mouth or by our letter" (2:15; cf. 3:6).

Yet the author deserves some credit for his adaptation of Paul since, in applying the gospel to the concrete problems of his church, he closely imitates Paul's hermeneutical method. In a situation in which apocalyptic excitement causes unrest so that some Christians have already abandoned their daily work, the author teaches his church that the apocalyptic timetable that he issues in the name of Paul demands an attitude of patient endurance and normal commitment to work.

Nevertheless, 2 Thessalonians does not represent an imaginative imitation of Paul. His duplication of Paul's letter to the Thessalonians turns his letter into an anachronistic product. And his eschatological teaching in 2:1-12 diverges so much from what Paul would have said, had he lived in the time and circumstances of the author of 2 Thessalonians, that his adaptation of Paul must be characterized as a pseudo-imitation of Paul.

And so his procedure cautions the church today that an appropriation of Paul's legacy is illegitimate and irrelevant when it supplements a literal borrowing from Paul's gospel with some up-to-date supplementary additions. Although it may seemingly edify our churches to hear the real Paul of old, this type of adaptation must be characterized as a perversion of the basic intent of Paul's gospel. Indeed, Paul's gospel wants to be a viva vox for those contingent problems and situations that preoccupy people in their present daily life.

*The Book of Acts*

In view of the extensive discussion of the person and function of Paul in Acts (see pp. 48–57, above), the remarks here will be limited to the adaptation of Luke's portrait of Paul by the church today.

We must realize that Acts forms a special case among Paul's interpreters in the New Testament. After all, it is a narrative about Paul instead of a pseudepigraphical letter in the name of Paul. As we saw, Luke intends to describe the history of the apostolic church in its mission from Jerusalem to Rome and wants to champion its unity, to defend its theological legitimacy over against Judaism, and to demonstrate its political innocence to Rome.

Although Luke gives the person and mission of Paul a central place in his narrative, he subordinates Paul's portrait to his larger apologetic purpose. Moreover, his portrayal of Paul is not based on Paul's letters but rather on oral traditions and legends about Paul. And so Luke concentrates on the greatness of Paul's personality and missionary accomplishments while he ignores the particularity of Paul's gospel.

Paul's adaptation by Luke, then, constitutes a grandiose rewriting of Pauline tradition and is a misguided attempt to refashion Paul to conform him to Luke's ideological presuppositions.

In the light of Luke's deformation of Pauline tradition, the high esteem in which the Paul of Acts is held by the church today can only be attributed to its lack of spiritual discernment.

Indeed, Luke's moralistic and pious temper may well be the reason for the heavy concentration on the Paul of Acts by Christian education curricula in our churches. To be sure, Acts offers us an easy guide to the life and career of Paul (see "the three missionary journeys"), but even in matters of chronology and the details of Paul's life its statements are often misleading, if not incorrect (see J. Knox).

And yet we can readily understand why Luke's two-volume work is so popular in our churches. It not only forms a continuous narrative, but also manifests a deep religious humanitarian sensitivity, in which piety and moralism are often conjoined (see, especially, Luke's parables). Acts enhances this moralistic posture of Luke's Gospel in several ways. For instance, it narrates the miracles performed by the "great men," Peter and Paul, and describes not only a series of Paul's miraculous escapes from dangerous situations but also his impressive rhetoric and especially his astonishing missionary accomplishments. However, when the church today adopts the pious, harmonious, and great personality of the Paul of Acts and subsequently attempts to harmonize this portrait of Paul with Paul's self-portrait in his letters, it not only confounds the members of our churches but also betrays the historical Paul.

## *Paul's Legacy for the Church Today*

After evaluating the adaptation of Paul's gospel by his early interpreters in the New Testament, it is time to focus specifically on the possibility of adapting Paul for the church today. Subsequently, it will be discussed to what extent these early interpreters of Paul in the New Testament can provide us with guidelines and prescriptions for our own adaptive work (see pp. 122–124, below).

### OPTIONS FOR THE CHURCH TODAY

Options for adapting Paul's legacy in the church today can be delineated as follows: (1) a traditionalist adaptation; (2)

a wholesale neglect and deconstruction of the tradition; and (3) an adaptation that acknowledges the burden of the tradition.

The first option considers the transliteration of the tradition the only way to be faithful to Paul's gospel. Here, the old text is simply reproduced and is made to fit new situations for which it was not intended (see pp. 119–120, below).

The second option rejects the need for a proper adaptation of the tradition. It represents an ahistorical and anachronistic stance because it dehistoricizes the old text by divorcing it from its original context. Thus it imposes on the text a subjective ideological reading that supposedly must meet the demands of the present time (see pp. 120–122, below).

The third option recognizes that the old text necessarily is subject to changes in its itinerary through time. This recognition can take two shapes: it can be formulated in either a "soft" way or a "hard" way.

The first form—the "soft" way—concentrates on Paul's method instead of his message because its proponents are convinced that the historicity of Paul's conceptuality makes it impossible to transpose his message to the so different historical circumstances of later times. However, advocates of this view believe that it opens up an attractive and viable alternative that is able to safeguard Paul's essential importance for the church today. Contrary to the time-conditioned character of the message of Paul's gospel, his hermeneutical method is considered to be universally relevant.

Indeed, we must acknowledge that this focus on Paul's method is an important reversal of the history of interpretation of Paul's gospel, which has tended to focus exclusively on the content of Paul's message. Moreover, it signifies an innovative and challenging form of adaptation because it is the task of every interpreter of Paul's gospel to imitate his method, i.e., to make the abiding word of the gospel a word on target for its audience. Indeed, an adaptation of the gospel that speaks the language of its hearers and is couched within their worldview qualifies in many ways as a faithful imitation of Paul because it conforms

to Paul's own conviction that the gospel has transforming power
only when it addresses the contemporary needs of its audiences.
However, notwithstanding the attractive features of this
"soft" form of adaptation, its deficiencies are apparent. The
"hard" form of adaptation correctly points out that it is not
permissible to sever Paul's method from his message because
message and method constitute an inseparable entity. Just as
there cannot be a message without a method, so there cannot
be a method without a message. Indeed, the integral relation of
Paul's method to the particularity of his message forbids us to
limit our adaptation of his gospel exclusively to his method.

To be sure, we must realize that this aggravates the problem of the viability of Paul's message for the church today. If
Paul's message is confined to its own dated historical world,
how is it possible to adapt it successfully to entirely new historical
circumstances?

## THE ADAPTATION OF PAUL'S GOSPEL
## IN THE CHURCH TODAY

To be sure, we must remember that there are times when
the problem of historicity seems to vanish. Appropriate analogies
may occur when Paul's images and symbols are able to appeal
directly to the imagination of the interpreter. For instance, Luther
discovered a direct analogy between the crisis situations of his
time and those of the Pauline era. And so he successfully adapted
Paul's image of justification by faith—which Paul originally had
forged in his anti-Judaizer polemic—to the legalistic practices
of the Roman Catholic church in the sixteenth century A.D.
Likewise he adapted Paul's antienthusiastic arguments against
the Corinthians in his own polemic against the left-wing Re-
formers (the *Schwärmer*). Indeed, church history furnishes us
with many examples of such direct analogies between past and
present historical eras.

However, we must realize that theologians and preachers
frequently construe misplaced and artificial analogies between

the past and the present in their attempt to adapt Paul's situation-specific language to our time. Such a fusion of Paul's first-century A.D. language with that of our time produces anomalous and arbitrary adaptations, which turn the realism of the imaginative into a form of the fanciful and fantastic. Green's observation that "the distinction between realistic and illusory use of imagination is a fundamental feature of the concept"[8] puts us on guard lest the imaginative slips into the imaginary. Popular adaptations, which take up misleading analogies and so misrepresent Paul's gospel (see pp. 103–4, above), have already been discussed.

Related to these misleading adaptations are misplaced adaptations: they construe an erroneous analogy between Paul's gospel and our time. Here the often remarkable exegetical depth of insight into the historical dimension of Paul's gospel is not matched by a proper hermeneutical bridge to the present. The normativity of the *sola scriptura* principle preoccupies these interpreters to such an extent that they simply equate the problems of Paul's time with those of our time. Thus they ignore the basic insight that is inherent in the process of adaptation, namely, that the Pauline text is subject to fundamental changes in its journey through time.

For example, Barth construes such a misplaced and artificial analogy between Paul's past and our present time when he interprets Paul's polemic against the works of the law in Romans as a polemic against the *homo religiosus* and against religiosity in general. This adaptation fails on two counts, since he erroneously suggests not only that religiosity forms the substance of Paul's argument in Romans, but also that this is the truly crucial problem of our time.

In contrast to these artificial analogies, Paul Tillich's interpretation of Paul's language of justification and grace provides us with a good example of an imaginative analogy, i.e., of a creative adaptation of Paul's gospel. The issue here is not whether we agree or disagree with Tillich's overall theological program. What is important is that Tillich understands the urgency of the task of adapting Paul for the concerns of the church today. Thus he attempts to transpose Paul's images of sin and grace into images that touch the experience of people today. Tillich senses the symbolic power of Paul's images as evinced in these words from a sermon: "There are few words more strange to most of us than 'sin' and 'grace.' They are strange, just because they are so well-known. . . . We must seriously ask ourselves whether we should use them at all, or whether we should discard them as useless tools. But there is a mysterious fact about the great words of our religious tradition; they cannot be replaced."

Tillich then adapts Paul's language by correlating sin with separation and grace with reunion and concludes his sermon by interpreting Paul's language of grace and justification in terms of the reality of God's "acceptance."[9]

After this brief perusal of some successful and some misguided adaptations of Paul's gospel, attention will be drawn to two forms of distorted adaptations that occupy center stage today. These pseudo-adaptations of Paul's gospel engage in a wholesale neglect and deconstruction of the tradition (see p. 116, above: the second adaptive option); they therefore differ from adaptations that, in one way or another, acknowledge the need for adaptation (see p. 116, above, options one and three). In other words, advocates of these pseudo-adaptations attempt to solve questions of the challenge of Paul's gospel in the church today by actually disowning the challenge. However, we must note that they adopt radically opposite methods for doing so.

A first type of such a pseudo-adaptation in the church today is the attempt to define faithfulness to Paul as the literal reproduction and transliteration of his gospel. This fundamentalistic conception of adaptation conforms to its view of the Bible as an inerrant and infallible book, which contains both historical veracity and timeless dogmatic truth. We must be aware that this conviction is not limited to fundamentalistic churches, since it also pervades many mainline Protestant churches in the form of what James Barr calls a "naïve fundamentalism,"[10] or what J. A. T. Robinson has called "the conservatism of the committed."[11]

Thus when mainline Protestant churches believe that the authority of Paul's gospel consists in the literal reproduction of its wording and conceptuality, they in fact substitute transliteration for adaptation. Such a procedure reifies Paul's language and treats his gospel as a frozen, eternally valid, dogmatic deposit. It imposes on the church a collage of Paul's statements, which come across as objects from outer space since the basic historicity of Paul's language is here ignored. Since Paul's formulations here constitute an indelible part of an infallible canon, their truly "biblical" status stipulates their uncontestable authority.

Although this procedure intends to facilitate the adaptation of Paul's legacy, its rigid conception of that legacy is in sharp conflict with Paul's own theological purpose. As we have seen, Paul's method of interweaving coherence and contingency does not tolerate a divorce between these two poles of his gospel. Thus fundamentalism's adoption of this bifurcation actually perverts what it so eagerly wants to preserve. Moreover, fundamentalism misunderstands what the notion of the continuity of the tradition involves. Since Paul attempts to proclaim the continuity of the gospel amid the discontinuity of its historical contingencies by adapting it to the circumstances and needs of its hearers, his procedure compels us to imitate him amid the radically new contingencies of our time.

A second type of such a pseudo-adaptation is advocated by some liberation theologians; it favors a method that represents the extreme opposite of the fundamentalistic stance. It revolves around recent hermeneutical discussions that reflect on the interaction between text and interpreter. For instance, "reader-response" criticism and the notion of *Wirkungsgeschichte* (the history of textual effects) have shown that traditional texts not only permit but even necessitate a multiplicity of readings because every new reading involves a fresh interaction between text and reader. Hans Gadamer's hermeneutical proposal of a fusion of horizons between text and reader, that brings about a new mutual understanding, has strongly influenced discussion of "the postmodern use of the Bible."[12] Indeed, the multiplicity of the readings, which every new reading of the text produces, is in some ways quite analogous to the variety of Paul's adaptations by his early interpreters in the New Testament.

However, the radical form of adaptation by some liberation theologians actually represents a gross misappropriation of the tradition. Rather than reproducing and imposing the old tradition on the modern situation, here the claim of the original tradition is evaporated for the sake of the claims of modernity. For instance, although Elisabeth Schüssler-Fiorenza correctly criticizes the androcentric legacy of the biblical and theological tradition and calls for its radical reconstruction, her hermeneutical proposals amount to a rejection of the normative character of the biblical text. She writes:

> Feminist theology therefore challenges biblical theological scholarship to develop a paradigm for biblical revelation that does not understand the New Testament as an archetype but as a prototype. Both archetype and prototype denote original models. However, an archetype is an ideal form that establishes an unchanging timeless pattern, whereas a prototype is not a binding timeless pattern or principle.
>
> A prototype, therefore, is critically open to the possibility of its own transformation. . . . Such an understanding of Scripture not as a mythic archetype but as a historical prototype provides the Christian community with a sense of its ongoing history as well as of its theological identity. Insofar as it does not define the Bible as a fixed mythical pattern it is able to acknowledge positively the dynamic process of biblical adaptation, challenge, or renewal of social-ecclesial and conceptual structures under the changing conditions of the church's social-historical situations."[13]

Whereas according to her definition "archetype" refers to the normative dimension of the text, "prototype" views the authority of the text in terms of a first instance, which is open to radical transformation. Although Schüssler-Fiorenza speaks in this context about "the dynamic process of biblical adaptation," adaptation is here not understood as a method to maintain the continuity of the tradition amid the discontinuities of historical change, but rather as the elimination and dismissal of the original claim of the tradition. Thus, since the authority of the biblical text is here limited to its prototypical status, the normative character of the biblical text is eroded. And we must recognize that this erosion affects as well the distinctive identity of the church as the community that derives its life from its interpretation of the biblical tradition.

All of these pseudo-adaptations have a common denominator, namely, their propensity to misrepresent or disregard the basic claims of Paul's original gospel. Thus they compel us to reflect on what constitutes an authentic adaptation of Paul's gospel.

## TOWARD AN AUTHENTIC ADAPTATION OF PAUL'S GOSPEL IN THE CHURCH TODAY

Although the church today is not allowed to disregard or minimize the historicity of Paul's gospel, it is my conviction that this problem does not constitute an insurmountable obstacle to its authentic contemporary adaptation.

A closer analysis of the interface between Paul's method and message shows that his gospel has actually three distinct components that compose its particularity: (1) an abiding coherent core; (2) a contingent target; and (3) coherent strategies that serve to correlate the abiding core of the gospel and the demands of its contingent target.

The reciprocal interaction among these three components of Paul's gospel serves to give his gospel its incarnational depth and situational specificity. Indeed, the core of the gospel signifies its abiding and constant subject matter, which Paul summarizes in short phrases such as "Jesus Christ, and him crucified" (1 Cor 2:2); "Christ Jesus, who died, yes, who was raised, who is at the right hand of God" (Rom 8:34); "Jesus died and rose again" (1 Thess 4:14). It is therefore important to pay close attention to the manner in which Paul brings the core of the gospel to bear upon the contingent needs of his churches. He does so by devising imaginative strategies, which creatively mediate between the abiding truth of the gospel and its contingent relevance.

M. Eugene Boring points to these imaginative strategies when he remarks with respect to Paul's soteriology that "the range of Paul's soteriological language—that is, how inclusive it is—is not determined by propositional systematic consistency, nor by his developments in his theology, nor by the tension between depth and surface structures, but *by the demands of the central encompassing images within which his language functions*, images that necessarily involve him in conflicting language games."[14] Gerd Theissen supports this point when he states that Paul's language functions with an irreconcilable plurality of images, each of which has its own internal logic.[15] I have argued in a similar vein that "Paul interprets the coherent apocalyptic core of the gospel in a variety of metaphors that interact and interweave to form an organic whole, so that a developmental or atomistic analysis of the various metaphors bypasses his hermeneutical intent. His interpretation of the gospel cannot be hierarchically structured, as if there is one primary metaphor that dominates all the others."[16]

Therefore, when we attempt to adapt Paul for the church today, we must pay close attention to the metaphorical character of Paul's thought, i.e., to Paul the image maker instead of to Paul the thinker of coherent propositions. It is this feature of his theologizing that enables us to adapt him properly. Images, metaphors, and symbols have an inherent power to transcend their historical specificity and confinement and therefore are able to evoke new and appropriate symbolic universes in the readers of Paul's gospel.

It is contended here, then, that our adaptation of Paul is only a faithful imitation and reenactment of his gospel when it allows the picture language that is manifest in Paul's coherent strategies to execute its transparent power, so that his images and metaphors become carriers of new meaning for us. Indeed, metaphors do their proper work when their figures of speech reframe and restructure our routinized manner of perceiving reality.[17] And so the historical distance between the time of Paul and our time can only be overcome, when—as said before (see p. 31, above)—we are able to transpose the *Sachverhalt* (message) of his gospel in a new *Sprachgestalt* (language).

We must remember that Paul's own adaptation of the Christian tradition, which he had received from his predecessors (1 Cor 11:23; 15:3), unfolds itself in a host of creative and innovative metaphors because "he was able to see a depth in the tradition which others did not perceive previously in its radicality."[18] Indeed, the coherent center of Paul's gospel is a symbolic structure, centered in the apocalyptic significance of the symbols of the cross and resurrection. It is grounded in the primordial experience of his conversion and call and disperses itself into a variety of images and symbols that Paul deems appropriate for whatever the contingent situation requires. Thus symbols such as righteousness, justification, reconciliation, freedom, adoption, and being in Christ emerge out of Paul's imaginative reflection on the Christ event in the light of contingent situations.

Although Lessing's "ugly ditch" has made us aware of the temporal and cultural gaps between Paul's time and our time, and thus of the historicity of Paul's formulations of the gospel, his images possess a transcendent power that is able to kindle our own imagination. These images can become "luminous sentences" (H. Richard Niebuhr) that, because of their multivalent character, profoundly impact our experience.

Whereas for Norman Perrin a symbol such as "the kingdom of God" evokes a myth,[19] I would suggest that Paul's symbols and images evoke the heart of his gospel. His gospel centers in the transforming power of God's action in Christ, i.e. in God's redemptive involvement in the life of his creation and in the promise of its glorious eschatological destiny.

## OUR COMMON TASK

This study has focused on the problems and challenges that Paul's legacy present to the church. It has argued that adaptation is not a free option but an unavoidable necessity if the church intends to remain faithful to Paul's gospel.

The early reception of Paul's gospel by the early New Testament interpreters demonstrates the necessity of adapting Paul's gospel for new times in history. Moreover, it shows not only the multiple adaptive strategies that these authors employed, but also the many risks and difficulties that the process of adaptation involves.

Paul's first interpreters in the history of the church, then, offer us important models and guidelines for our task of transmitting Paul's gospel. Although our sociocultural circumstances, worldviews, and constructions of reality differ considerably from those of Paul's first-century A.D. interpreters, adaptation continues to be our common task. Indeed, our investigation of Paul's early interpreters has clearly shown how difficult it was for them to adapt Paul's gospel properly, especially because of the constraints that the historical circumstances of their time forced upon them. Thus they sound a warning to us not to be captivated by the many pseudo-adaptations of Paul's gospel that have dominated Paul's exegesis in the history of the church and that still prevail in the church today.

The twofold method proposed in this study (see pp. 16–17, above) aims to clarify the intricate relation between the original claim of the tradition and its necessary transposition to the changed situations and worldviews of later times. In fact, the comparative and the traditio-historical components of this method constitute a hermeneutical circle, which must verify how and to what extent the urgent claims of the "old" tradition can be upheld when they encounter the equally urgent claims of new historical circumstances. In this context it was suggested that adaptation is the indispensable tool of the traditio-historical method. Adaptation attempts to mediate between the claims of the past and those of the present, and resists both the literal transliteration of the past into the present and the dismissal of the tradition in favor of some modern *eis-egesis*.

Moreover, contrary to the historical and absolutizing tendencies of the comparative method, adaptation is sensitive to the historicity of the tradition and thus to the necessary transpositions of the tradition that its new environment demands.

However, the reader will ask: In what way are the adaptive efforts of Paul's early interpreters helpful to us in our attempt to adapt Paul's gospel for the contemporary church? Indeed, when we reflect on their frequent failures in properly adapting Paul's gospel, we are inclined to subscribe to the view that they represent indeed a fall from the true Paul.

However, we must realize that this judgment is based on a one-sided application of the comparative method. This method demonstrates an insensitive attitude to the historical dimensions of the problems involved in adaptation and in the transmission of tradition. Even in their failures the early interpreters of Paul provide the church today with important guidelines and warning signals.

In the first place, they teach us that adaptation cannot be avoided but remains a necessary task in every new period of the church's life if Paul's gospel is to remain a living word for new times and seasons. Thus we must remember that the importance of their contribution does not so much consist in their successes, but rather in their conviction that a true imitation of Paul necessitates the adaptation of his gospel to new historical circumstances.

Secondly, they teach us that the necessity of adaptation involves a heavy burden. It is the burden of coming to terms with the particularity of Paul's gospel, i.e., with Paul's situation-specific hermeneutic. As we have seen, the particularity of Paul's theological method and message produces almost insuperable obstacles to the adequate adaptation of his gospel. And thus we must refrain from making apodictic statements that show no empathy for the burdens Paul's later pupils faced.

Thirdly, they put us on notice that the adaptation of a renowned "canonical" figure by later generations is always in danger of accepting uncritically his "holy" legacy. In other words, grateful reverence for the memory of Paul and his impact on church history causes us to blur the real portrait of Paul.

Fourthly, although the comparative method compels us to disapprove many of the adaptive products of these early interpreters, we should be aware that their adaptive methods to a large extent still permeate our contemporary adaptations of Paul. For instance, we may blame the *P.E.* for their rigid presentation of Paul's teaching and for turning Paul into an organization man; we may scold 2 Thessalonians for its anachronistic repetition of Paul's teaching and its feeble effort to update Paul's eschatological teaching; and we may consider Acts to be an ideological rewrite of Pauline tradition.

However, we also must remember that we often greatly appreciate the simple Paul of the *P.E.*, not in the least because he seems so much more practical in sustaining church order than the impractical historical Paul. Moreover, we frequently imitate 2 Thessalonians when we desire to be as faithful as possible to the real historical Paul and yet want to increase his relevance with some updating comments.

Moreover, the almost exclusive focus of our churches on Luke's portrait of Paul is less commendable than what Luke did. Whereas Luke felt constrained to save the revolutionary Paul—the beloved apostle of gnostic heretics—for the apostolic church of his time, we do not have such an excuse when we favor so heavily Luke's portrait of Paul. Furthermore, we tend to disregard the adaptive strategies of Ephesians and Colossians because we often present these letters simply as authentic writings of the historical Paul and do not treat them for what they really are, i.e., truly imaginative and creative products of his later pupils.

And, finally, we must realize that—except for Acts—almost all the pseudepigraphical Pauline letters sense that the essence of Paul's gospel is grounded in his hermeneutical method of conjoining the abiding truth of the gospel to situation-specific contingencies. And although most of them misconstrued Paul's method because they were influenced too much by the catholicizing trend of their days, they invite us to learn from their mistakes and successes and challenge us to create a more adequate adaptation of Paul's gospel.

It has been suggested here that the evocative power of Paul's images and metaphors enable us to adapt Paul in an appropriate and relevant manner to the circumstances of our time.

Although originally addressed to different historical periods and places, these images and metaphors of Paul have the power to pierce through the limitations of time and to kindle our own creative adaptations.

Thus the adaptation of Paul's gospel by the church today should perhaps more closely resemble the imaginative and creative process undertaken by a composer who takes a theme from a previous era and allows it to speak in the musical idiom of his or her own day—as Bach set the Reformation chorales in his cantatas and passions, or as a jazz musician improvises on a classic theme. In each case, a creative and skillful composer or musician maintains the integrity of the original motif yet allows its emotive and communicative power to come through in the hearer's own musical language. The challenge and mandate to the church today is to engage in a similar creative act. May it so reenact the powerful word of Paul's gospel that it transforms our lives today in the same way it transformed those who heard it in the past.

# NOTES

## CHAPTER 1

1. Henceforth the term "post-Pauline writings" will be used to refer to the writings of his pupils in the New Testament, i.e., to the deutero-Pauline letters and Acts. Thus James and 2 Peter—the other interpreters of Paul in the New Testament—are not discussed.

2. See Dibelius and Conzelmann, *The Pastoral Epistles*.

3. *Introduction to the New Testament*, 384.

4. *Geschichte der urchristlichen Literatur*, 232; author's translation.

5. *Die sogenannten Pastoralbriefe des Apostels Paulus aufs neue kritisch untersucht*; author's translation.

6. "Pastoralbriefe," in *RGG* iv, (3d ed.), p. 994; author's translation.

7. " 'Pfeiler und Fundament der Wahrheit': Erwägungen zum Kirchenverständnis der Pastoralbriefe," in *Kümmel-Festschrift*, 229; author's translation.

8. Ibid., 229.

9. In W. A. Meeks, ed., *The Writings of St. Paul*.

10. 434; the emphasis has been added by this author.

11. Søren Kierkegaard, *Philosophical Fragments*.

12. On this issue, see Ben C. Ollenburger, "What Krister Stendahl Meant. A Normative Critique of Descriptive Biblical Theology," *Horizons in Biblical Theology* 8 (1986) 61–98.

13. Ibid., 213.

14. Ebeling, *The Problem of Historicity*, 22, 23, 25–27.

15. Cf., for instance, R. Wilken, *The Myth of Christian Beginnings.*

# CHAPTER 2

1. Proposal for SBL Meeting, Atlanta, 1986, 2.

2. Quoted in J. C. Beker, "Paul's Theology: Consistent or Inconsistent," 369–70.

3. Cf. K. Berger, "Die Impliziten Gegner. Zur Methode des Erschliessens von Gegnern in neutestamentlichen Texten."

4. Yeager, "Passion and Suspicion: Religious Affections in 'The Will To Believe.' " *JR* 69 (1989): 473.

5. Ibid., 471.

6. Ibid., 475.

7. Ibid., 485.

8. Cf. J. B. Lightfoot, *Notes on Epistles of St. Paul*, 15.

9. Cf. V. Furnish, who notes that this is "by far the most elaborate instance of the use of military imagery in the Pauline letters" (*II Corinthians*, 457).

10. Cf. also Rom 15:5-6; 1 Cor 8:6; Phil 2:11.

11. *Paul, the Law, and the Jewish People*, 70; see also 88 n. 24.

12. Cf. Tertullian, for whom Paul was "the apostle of the heretics," (*Adv. Marcion* 3.5).

13. "The Particularity of the Pauline Epistles as a Problem in the Ancient Church," *Cullmann-Festschrift*, 1962, 261.

14. Ibid., 271.

15. Even Luther, who questioned the adequacy of James and Revelation, never disputed the essential harmony of the apostolic witness in the New Testament.

# CHAPTER 3

1. *P.E.* = Pastoral Epistles.

2. K. M. Fischer, "Anmerkungen zur Pseudepigraphie im Neuen Testament," 76.

3. It is unlikely that the author of the *P.E.* knew the complete collection of Paul's letters. Regional circulation of some of his letters must

be distinguished from the latter collection of the total Pauline corpus
(cf. L. Mowry, "The Early Circulation of Paul's Letters").
   4. K. H. Schelkle, *Das Neue Testament: Eine Einführung,* 183; cf.
also N. Brox, *Die Pastoralbriefe,* 74.
   5. J. Roloff, *Apostolat, Verkündigung, Kirche,* 274–75.
   6. Notice the frequent occurrence of Pauline terms such as the
following: "faith" (*[pistis]*); 32x); "in [the] faith" (*en pistei* 1 Tim
1:2, 4; 2:7, 15; 3:13; 4:12; 2 Tim 1:13; Titus 1:13; 3:15); "to believe/
entrust" (*[pisteuein]* 1 Tim 1:16; 3:16; 2 Tim 1:12; Titus 1:3; 3:8);
"righteous/just" (*[dikaios]* 1 Tim 1:9; 2 Tim 4:8; Titus 1:8; 2:12);
"to justify/vindicate" (*[dikaioun]* 1 Tim 3:16; Titus 3:7); "righteousness" (*[dikaiosynē]* 1 Tim 6:11; 2 Tim 2:22; 3:16; 4:8; Titus 3:5);
"love" (*[agapē]* 1 Tim 5:14; 2:15; 4:12; 6:11; 2 Tim 1:7, 13; 2:22;
3:10; Titus 2:2, 10); "to love" (*[agapein]* 2 Tim 4:8, 10); "beloved"
(*[agapētos]* 1 Tim 6:2; 2 Tim 1:2); "hope/to hope" (*[elpis/elpizein* 1
Tim 1:1; Titus 1:2; 2:13; 3:7; 1 Tim 3:14; 4:10; 5:5; 6:17); "to
save" (*[sōzein]* 1 Tim 1:15; 2:4, 15; 4:16; 2 Tim 1:9; 4:18; Titus
3:5); "grace" (*[charis]* 1 Tim 1:2, 14; 6:21; 2 Tim 1:2, 9; 2:1; 4:22;
Titus 1:4; 2:11; 3:7,15); "peace" (*[eirēnē]* 1 Tim 1:2; 2 Tim 1:2;
2:22; Titus 1:4); "to urge/exhort" (*[parakalein]* 1 Tim 1:3; 2:1; 5:1;
6:2; 2 Tim 4:2; Titus 1:9; 2:6, 15); also "exhortation" (*[paraklesis]*
1 Tim 4:13). To this list we can add the close similarity of the letter-
openings and -closings to those of Paul.
   7. Cf. Kümmel, *Introduction to the NT,* 382.
   8. The noun and verb "to appear" (*[epiphaneia]*; *[epiphainein]*)
can also refer to God (Titus 2:11; 3:4) or to both God and Christ
(Titus 2:13); moreover, the noun and verb can refer either to the
incarnation of Christ (2 Tim 1:10, cf. Titus 2:11; 3:4) or to his future
parousia (1 Tim 6:14; 2 Tim 4:1, 2; Titus 2:13).
   9. Such as the following; "piety"/"godliness" (*eusebeia,* 1 Tim 2:2;
4:7, 8; 6:3, 4, 5, 11; 2 Tim 3:5; Titus 1:1); "the teaching," "doctrine"
(*didaskalia,* 1 Tim 4:6; 6:3); "sound doctrine" (*hygiainousa didaskalia,* 1 Tim 1:10; 2 Tim 4:3; Titus 1:9; 2:1); "the sound words"
(*hygiainontes logoi,* 1 Tim 6:3; 2 Tim 1:13; cf. "to be sound" (*hy-
giainein,* Titus 1:13; 2:2); "serious"/"seriousness," "gravity" (*semnos/
semnotes,* 1 Tim 3:8, 11; Titus 2:2/ 1 Tim 2:2; 3:4; Titus 2:7); "a
good or clear conscience" (*agathe* or *kathara syneidēsis* 1 Tim 1:5,
19; 3:9; 2 Tim 1:3; cf. also 1 Tim 4:2; Titus 1:15); "knowledge of
the truth" (*epignosis aletheias,* 1 Tim 2:4; 2 Tim 2:25, 3:7; Titus 1:1;

cf. also "truth" (*aletheia*, 1 Tim 2:7; 3:15; 4:3; 6:5; 2 Tim 2:15, 18; 3:8; 4:4; Titus 1:14); "to train"/"training" (*paideuein/paideia*, 1 Tim 1:20; 2 Tim 2:25; Titus 2:12/2 Tim 3:16).
10. Ibid., 383.
11. Ibid., 373.
12. *The Pastoral Epistles*, 39.
13. *Die Pastoralbriefe*, 124.
14. Ibid., 40–41.
15. Ibid., 125.
16. V. Hasler, *Die Briefe an Timotheus und Titus*, 68; quoted in Brox, ibid., 39.
17. In accordance with the prevelant nomenclature, I call the author of Acts "Luke."
18. *Chapters in a Life of Paul*, 92.
19. See *The Apostolic Preaching and Its Development*.
20. See, for example, Ernst Käsemann, Philipp Vielhauer, and Siegfried Schuz.
21. "Die Paulus-Darstellung des Lukas," 524.
22. For the reason behind Luke's elaborate apology for Paul, see pp. 61–63, below.
23. Robert C. Tannehill, *The Narrative Unity of Luke-Acts: A Literary Interpretation*, vol. 1, xiii.
24. Cf. *boulē tou theou* in Luke 7:30; Acts 2:23; 4:28; 5:38-39; 13:36; 20:27; *dei* in Luke 24:7, 26, 44; Acts 9:16; 14:22; 17:3; 19:21; 23:11; 27:24.
25. The point of the story of 8:9-24 is the superiority of the gospel over magicians like Simon; 8:24 shows that the confrontation with magicians continues to be an issue for the church (cf. also 13:6, 8; 16:6-18); cf. Susan Garrett, *The Demise of the Devil: Magic and the Demonic in Luke's Writings*.
26. *Die Apostelgeschichte*, 302 (author's translation).
27. I owe this suggestion to my graduate student, James S. Hanson.
28. Cf., for instance, the charge against the asocial behavior of Christians in 16:16-22 and 19:23-40.
29. See Col 1:6, 9, 11, 15, 18-20, 23, 28; 2:2, 22; 3:8, 14, 17, 20, 22; 4:7, 12.
30. H. Conzelmann, "Paulus und die Weisheit."
31. Notice the emphasis in the last line of the epistle: "Remember my chains" (*mou tōn desmōn*, 4:18); cf. also the ending of Ephesians: "the gospel, for which I am an ambassador in chains (*hyper hou presbeuō en halusei*, Eph 6:20).

32. See *The Romans Debate*, 144.

33. *Notes on the Epistles of St. Paul*; cf. also Leander Keck: "the most mature statement of Paul's theology" (*Paul and His Letters*, 4).

34. See *Paul: Apostle of the Heart Set Free.*

35. Jack T. Sanders, "Hymnic Elements in Ephesians 1–3."

36. See the unusually long syntax constructions of Eph 1:3-14, 1:15, 23; 2:1-7, 3:1-7, 14-19; 4:11-16; 5:7-13; 6:14-20.

37. Schnackenburg, *Der Brief an die Epheser*, 20.

38. R. F. Collins, *Letters That Paul Did Not Write*, 219.

39. Ibid., 227.

40. Ibid., 232.

41. Ibid., 237.

42. Cf. 2 Tim 1:13 (*hypotyposos*); also Col 1:24, 29; 2:1; Eph 4:1.

43. 2 Thess 3:4, 6, 14, 17; 1 Tim 1:11-17; 2 Tim 1:11-14; Col 1:24, 25; Eph 3:1-10.

44. Ibid., 240.

# CHAPTER 4

1. Ernst Käsemann, "The Canon of the New Testament."

2. However, my emphasis on the tradition-process does not subscribe to the view of a simple continuing development, as proposed by many Roman Catholic scholars (cf., for example, Heinrich Schlier).

3. Acts, of course, constitutes a special case, since it is a narrative about Paul, embedded in a comprehensive account of the history of the apostolic church at the close of the first century A.D.

4. "Theologie und Seelsorge aus Paulinischer Tradition: Einfuhrung in 2 Thess, Kol, Eph," 100; author's translation.

5. *The Pastoral Epistles*, 40–41.

6. Cf. D. R. MacDonald, *The Legend and the Apostle: The Battle for Paul in Story and Canon.*

7. "Amt, Kirche und Theologie in der nachapostolischen Epoche," 126; author's translation.

8. Ibid., 132.

9. Ibid., 123.

10. Cf. W. G. Kümmel, *Introduction*, 352–56.

11. "False Presuppositions in the Study of Romans," 144.

12. *Paul and His Letters*, 4.

13. *Paul, Apostle of the Heart Set Free*, 424.

14. Cf. Harry Gamble, *The Textual History of the Letter to the Romans: A Study in Textual and Literary Criticism.*

15. Cf. J. C. Beker, *Paul the Apostle,* 303–18.

16. Cf. Charles H. Talbert, *Luke and the Gnostics: An Examination of the Lucan Purpose,* 1966.

17. See note 18 for the special case of Acts.

18. Although Acts shares many features of this list, it deviates from the pseudepigraphal Pauline letters on points 1, 4, and possibly 7.

19. "Häresie und Einheit der Kirche im 2. Jahrhundert."

20. Quoted in Adolf von Harnack, *History of Dogma,* 1:89.

21. *Paulusverständis,* 119–20; author's translation.

# CHAPTER 5

1. *Theologie und Verkündigung,* 55, no. 6; author's translation.

2. Found in Brown, *Life Against Death.*

3. Scroggs, *Paul for a New Day,* 25.

4. "Amt, Kirche und Theologie," 123 (author's translation).

5. The adaptations of Paul by James and 2 Peter are not discussed in this study because, although these writings refer to and comment on Paul's letters, they neither pretend to be pupils of Paul (as do the pseudepigraphical Pauline letters) nor cast Paul in a heroic role (as does Acts).

6. Bruce M. Metzger, *The New Testament: Its Background, Growth and Contents* (Nashville: Abingdon, 1965).

7. Luke T. Johnson, *The Writings of the New Testament,* 374.

8. Garret Green, *Imagining God,* 63.

9. Ibid., 162.

10. *The Shaking of the Foundations,* 153.

11. J. Barr, *Fundamentalism,* 334.

12. J. A. T. Robinson, *Can We Trust the New Testament?,* 25.

13. Cf. Edgar V. McKnight, *Postmodern Use of the Bible.*

14. *In Memory of Her,* 33, 34.

15. "The Language of Universal Salvation in Paul," 275 (emphasis added).

16. "Soteriologische Symbolik in den paulinischen Schriften."

17. *Paul the Apostle,* 260.

18. On this issue, cf. S. J. Kraftchick, "Metaphor as Redescription: II Cor 10:3-6."

19. Beker, *Paul the Apostle,* 127.

20. Cf. M. E. Boring, ibid., 291, no. 69.

# BIBLIOGRAPHY

Aleith, E. *Paulusverständnis*. Berlin: A. Toppelmann, 1937.

Barr, James. *Fundamentalism*. Philadelphia: Westminster Press, 1978.

Beker, J. Christiaan. *Paul the Apostle: The Triumph of God in Life and Thought*. 2d ed. Philadelphia: Fortress Press, 1984.

————. "Paul's Theology: Consistent or Inconsistent?" *NTS* 34 (1988): 364–77.

————. *The Triumph of God: The Essence of Paul's Thought*. Trans. Loren T. Stuckenbruck. Minneapolis: Fortress Press, 1990.

Berger, Klaus. "Die Impliziten Gegner. Zur Methode des Erschliessens von Gegnern in neutestamentlichen Texten." In *Kirche: Festschrift für Günther Bornkamm zum 75. Geburtstag*. Edited by Dieter Lührmann and Georg Strecker. Tübingen: Mohr, 1980, 373–400.

Boers, Hendrikus. Proposal for SBL Meeting, Atlanta (1986).

Boring, Eugene. "The Language of Universal Salvation in Paul." *JBL* 105 (1986): 269–92.

Brown, Norman Oliver. *Life Against Death: The Psychoanalytical Meaning of History*. Middletown, Conn.: Wesleyan University Press, 1970.

Brox, Norbert. "Amt, Kirche und Theologie in der nachapostolischen Epoche: Die Pastoralbriefe." In *Gestalt und Anspruch des Neuen Testaments*. Edited by J. Schreiner. Würzburg: Echter-Verlag, 1969, 120–33.

_____. *Die Pastoralbriefe*. Regensburger Neues Testament, Vol. 7:2. Regensburg: Verlag F. Pustet, 1969.

Bruce, F. F. *Paul: Apostle of the Heart Set Free*. Exeter: Paternoster Press, 1977.

Bultmann, Rudolf. "Pastoralbriefe." In *Die Religion in Geschichte und Gegenwart*. 2d ed. 5 vols. Tübingen: J.C.B. Mohr (Paul Siebeck), 1930, Vol. 4, 993–97.

Collins, R. F. *Letters That Paul Did Not Write: The Epistle to the Hebrews and the Pauline Pseudepigrapha*. Good News Studies 28. Wilmington, Del.: Michael Glazier, 1988.

Conzelmann, Hans. "Paulus und die Weisheit." In *Theologie als Schriftauslegung*. Munich: Kaiser, 1974, 77–90.

Dahl, Nils A. "The Particularity of the Pauline Epistles as a Problem in the Ancient Church." In *Neotestamenta et Patristica: Eine Freundesgabe, Herrn Prof. Dr. O. Cullmann zu seinem 60. Geburtstag. Nov. Test.* Supplements 6. Leiden: E. J. Brill, 1962, 261–71.

Dautzenberg, Gerhard. "Theologie und Seelsorge aus Paulinischer Tradition: Einführung in 2 Thess, Kol, Eph." In *Gestalt und Anspruch des Neuen Testaments*. Edited by J. Schreiner. Würzburg: Echter Verlag, 1969, 96–119.

Dibelius, Martin, and Hans Conzelmann. *The Pastoral Epistles*. Trans. by Phillip Buttolph and Adela Yarbro. Edited by Helmut Koester. Philadelphia: Fortress, 1972.

Dodd, C. H. *The Apostolic Preaching and Its Development*. 2d edition. New York: Harper & Row, 1951.

Donfried, Karl. "False Presuppositions in the Study of Romans." In *The Romans Debate*. Edited by Karl P. Donfried. Minneapolis: Augsburg, 1977, 120–48.

Ebeling, Gerhard. *The Problem of Historicity in the Church and Its Proclamation*. Translated by Grover Foley. Philadelphia: Fortress, 1967.

_____. *Theologie und Verkündigung: Hermeneutische Untersuchungen zur Theologie*. Tübingen: J.C.B. Mohr (Paul Siebeck), 1963.

Elze, Martin. "Häresie und Einheit der Kirche im 2. Jahrhundert." *Zeitschrift für Theologie und Kirche* 71 (1974):389–409.

Fischer, K. M. "Anmerkungen zur Pseudepigraphie im Neuen Testament." *NTS* 23 (1977): 76–79.

Furnish, Victor Paul. *II Corinthians*. Anchor Bible 32A. Garden City, N.Y.: Doubleday, 1984.

Gamble, Harry. *The Textual History of the Letter to the Romans: A Study in Textual and Literary Criticism*. Grand Rapids: Eerdmans, 1977.

Garrett, Susan R. *The Demise of the Devil. Magic and the Demonic in Luke's Writings*. Minneapolis: Fortress, 1989.

Green, Garrett. *Imagining God*. San Francisco: Harper & Row, 1989.

Harnack, Adolf von. *History of Dogma*. 3d ed. 7 vols. London: Williams and Norgate, 1895-1900.

Hübner, Hans. *Law in Paul's Thought: Studies in the New Testament and Its World*. Edinburgh: T. & T. Clark, 1983.

Johnson, Luke Timothy. *The Writings of the New Testament: An Interpretation*. Philadelphia: Fortress Press, 1986.

Käsemann, Ernst. "The Canon of the New Testament and the Unity of the Church." In *Essays on New Testament Themes*. Translated by W. J. Montague. Philadelphia: Fortress, 1982, 95–107.

————. "Paulus und der Frühkatholizismus." In *Exegetische Versuche und Besinnungen*. 2 volumes. Göttingen: Vandenhoeck & Ruprecht, 1964. Vol. 2, 239–52.

Keck, Leander. *Paul and His Letters*. Philadelphia: Fortress, 1979.

Kraftchick, Steven J. "Metaphor as Redescription: II Cor. 10:3-6." Paper presented at the Annual Meeting of the Society of Biblical Literature, 1990.

Kümmel, Werner Georg. *Introduction to the New Testament*. Trans. Howard C. Kee. Nashville: Abingdon, 1973.

Lightfoot, J. B. *Notes on Epistles of St. Paul from Unpublished Commentaries*. London and New York: MacMillan, 1895.

Kierkegaard, Søren. *Philosophical Fragments*. Trans. Howard Hong. Princeton, N.J.: Princeton University Press, 1962.

Knox, John. *Chapters in a Life of Paul*. Nashville: Abingdon-Cokesbury, 1950.

MacDonald, D. R. *The Legend and the Apostle: The Battle for Paul in Story and Canon*. Philadelphia: The Westminster Press, 1983.

McKnight, Edgar V. *Postmodern Use of the Bible*. Nashville: Abingdon, 1988.

Metzger, Bruce M. *The New Testament: Its Background, Growth and Content*. Nashville: Abingdon Press, 1965.

Mowry, L. "The Early Circulation of Paul's Letters." *JBL* 63 (1964): 73–86.

Ollenburger, Ben C. "What Krister Stendahl Meant. A Normative Critique of Descriptive Biblical Theology." *Horizons in Biblical Theology* 8 (1986): 61–98.

Robinson, J. A. T. *Can We Trust the New Testament?* Grand Rapids: Eerdmans, 1977.

Roloff, Jürgen. *Die Apostelgeschichte.* Das Neue Testament Deutsch 5. Göttingen: Vandenhoeck & Ruprecht, 1981.

_____. *Apostolat, Verkündigung, Kirche.* Gutersloh: Gutersloher Verlagshaus G. Mohn, 1965.

_____. "Die Paulus-Darstellung des Lukas. Ihre geschichtlichen Voraussetzungen und ihr theologisches Ziel." *Evangelische Theologie* 39 (1979):510–31.

_____. " 'Pfeiler und Fundament der Wahrheit': Erwägungen zum Kirchenverständnis der Pastoralbriefe." In *Glaube und Eschatologie: Festschrift für Werner Georg Kümmel zum 80. Geburtstag.* Edited by Erich Grässer and Otto Merk. Tübingen: Mohr, 1985, 373–400.

Sanders, E. P. *Paul, the Law, and the Jewish People.* Philadelphia: Fortress Press, 1983.

Schelkle, Karl H. *Das Neue Testament: Seine literarische und theologische Geschichte.* Kevelaer Rhineland: Butzon & Bercker, 1963.

Schnackenburg, Rudolf. *Der Brief an die Epheser.* Evangelisch-Katholischer Kommentar 10. Zurich: Benziger Verlag, 1982.

Schulz, Siegfried. *Die Mitte der Schrift: Der Frühkatholizismus im Neuen Testament als Herausforderung an den Protestantismus.* Stuttgart and Berlin: Kreuz-Verlag, 1976.

Schüssler-Fiorenza, Elisabeth. *In Memory of Her: A Feminist Theological Reconstruction of Christian Origins.* New York: Crossroad, 1983.

Scroggs, Robin. *Paul for a New Day.* Philadelphia: Fortress Press, 1977.

Stendahl, Krister. "The Apostle Paul and the Introspective Conscience of the West." In *The Writings of St. Paul.* Edited by Wayne A. Meeks. New York: W.W. Norton & Co., 1972, 422–34.

Talbert, Charles H. *Luke and the Gnostics: An Examination of the Lucan Purpose.* Nashville: Abingdon, 1966.

Tannehill, Robert C. *The Narrative Unity of Luke-Acts: A Literary Interpretation.* 2 volumes. Philadelphia: Fortress, 1986.

Theissen, Gerd. "Soteriologische Symbolik in den paulinischen Schriften." *Kerygma und Dogma* 20, 1974, 282–304.

Tillich, Paul. *The Shaking of the Foundations.* New York: Charles Scribner's Sons, 1948.

Vielhauer, Philipp. *Geschichte der urchristlichen Literatur.* Berlin: Walter de Gruyter, 1975.

————. "Zum 'Paulinismus' der Apostelgeschichte." In *Aufsätze zum Neuen Testament.* Munich: Chr. Kaiser Verlag, 1965.

Wilken, Robert. *The Myth of Christian Beginnings: History's Impact on Belief.* Garden City, N.Y.: Doubleday, 1971.

Yeager, D. M. "Passion and Suspicion: Religious Affections in 'The Will to Believe.' " *Journal of Religion* 69 (1989): 467–83.

# INDEX

## SCRIPTURE INDEX

# AUTHOR INDEX